Authors:

Kathryn Senior is a former biomedical research scientist who studied at Cambridge University for a degree and a doctorate in microbiology. After 4 years in research she joined the world of publishing as an editor of children's science books. She has now been a science writer for 20 years.

Brian Williams studied English at university and has taught in both primary and secondary education. He worked for *Encyclopaedia Britannica* for several years as editor of *Children's Britannica* before becoming a full-time writer.

Ian Graham studied applied physics at the City University, London. He then took a postgraduate degree in journalism, specialising in science and technology. Since becoming a freelance author and journalist, he has written well over a hundred children's non-fiction books.

Artist:

David Antram was born in Brighton, England, in 1958. He studied at Eastbourne College of Art and then worked in advertising for fifteen years before becoming a full-time artist. He has illustrated many children's non-fiction books.

Series creator:

David Salariya was born in Dundee, Scotland. He has illustrated a wide range of books and has created and designed many new series for publishers in the UK and overseas. David established The Salariya Book Company in 1989. He lives in Brighton, England, with his wife, illustrator Shirley Willis, and their son Jonathan.

Editors: Karen Barker Smith, Michael Ford

Editorial Assistants: Victoria England, Mark Williams

Visit our **new** online shop at
shop.salariya.com
for great offers, gift ideas, all our new releases and free postage and packaging.

PAPER FROM
SUSTAINABLE
FORESTS

Published in Great Britain in MMXII by
Book House, an imprint of
The Salariya Book Company Ltd
25 Marlborough Place, Brighton BN1 1UB
www.salariya.com
www.book-house.co.uk

ISBN-13: 978-1-908759-65-8

SALARIYA

1 3 5 7 9 8 6 4 2

A CIP catalogue record for this book is available from the British Library.

Printed and bound in China.

Visit our website at **www.book-house.co.uk**
or go to **www.salariya.com** for **free** electronic versions of:
You Wouldn't Want to be an Egyptian Mummy!
You Wouldn't Want to be a Roman Gladiator!
You Wouldn't Want to be a Polar Explorer!
You Wouldn't Want to sail on a 19th-Century Whaling Ship!

Previous editions: MMII, MMIII, MMIV

You Wouldn't Want to be Ill in Tudor Times! (MMII) (KS)
Published by Hodder Wayland, an imprint of Hodder Children's Books;
© The Salariya Book Company Ltd MMII

Faraday and the Science of Electricity (MMIII) (BW)
HB ISBN-13: 978-1-904194-87-3
PB ISBN-13: 978-1-904194-88-0

Bell and the Science of the Telephone (MMIV) (BW)
HB ISBN-13: 978-1-904642-51-0
PB ISBN-13: 978-1-904642-52-7

Curie and the Science of Radioactivity (MMIV) (IG)
HB ISBN-13: 978-1-904642-53-4
PB ISBN-13: 978-1-904642-54-1

The Wright Brothers and the Science of Flight (MMIII) (IG)
HB ISBN-13: 978-1-904194-89-7
PB ISBN-13: 978-1-904194-90-3

Trouble with Science

Written by
Ian Graham
Kathryn Senior
Brian Williams

Illustrated by
David Antram

Created and designed by
David Salariya

BOOK HOUSE

Contents

Pioneering Scientists

Who'd want to be a scientist or an inventor? You spend long years carrying out endless experiments which might never have the results you're hoping for. Your health could be ruined by germs or radiation; you could be killed – or kill someone else – in a dreadful accident. Why would anyone choose to lead this kind of life?

Inventing the Modern Age

This book tells the story of some people who did make that choice. They faced hardship, danger, even death, to carry out their work. And why was their work so important? Because it helped to shape the world we live in. Aircraft, telephones, electric power and radiotherapy are so familiar today that we cannot imagine life without them – but these things did not exist until some clever and energetic people invented them.

Science is not new. Our story starts in the 16th century, when many people still believed in witchcraft – yet already there were scientists carefully studying human anatomy, observing the effects of herbs and drugs, laying the foundations of the modern science of medicine. That's how science works: each person builds on the discoveries of those who went before.

So, What Is a Scientist?

A scientist is a person who is curious about the world – a person who is determined to understand how things work, and why.

Could you be such a person?

5

You Wouldn't Want to Be a Pioneer of Medicine

Introduction

Your name is Nicholas Knight, and you are a barber surgeon in the 16th century, known in England as Tudor times. You were born in 1533, the same year as Queen Elizabeth I. Cities and towns in Tudor times are overcrowded and filthy. Animals live in houses, and waste is slopped straight into the street. It is no great surprise that people often get ill. When they do, there are no hospitals or doctors with a choice of medicines. The medicine that is available is weird and sometimes horrifying.

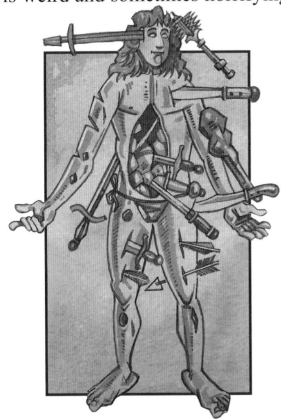

Your father is eager for you to be an important man in society. You showed an early interest in learning, so you have been sent to London at the age of twelve to become a barber surgeon's apprentice. London is an exciting place, but as you begin to learn the craft of medicine, you soon learn why you wouldn't want to be ill in the 16th century!

A Tough Start

You arrive in London to work with your master in 1545, when you are twelve years old. You have to share a room in your master's house with another young apprentice. You spend long days reading your master's books and listening to him talk about his work. After a few weeks, he decides to take you out to see the sick.

One way to diagnose illnesses is to examine patients' urine. Your master uses a collection of glass pots to examine the urine three times: once when it is fresh, again when it has cooled for about an hour, and then when it is completely cold. Sometimes you even have to taste the urine to see if it is sweet or sour!

What You Will Need

GLASS POTS in which to examine the urine. You hold the pot up to the light to see its colour and to see if it contains any particles. You then consult a book (below) to make a diagnosis.

A COLOUR WHEEL that you use to compare the colour of the urine. The colours are linked to different types of illnesses.

Glass pot

Padua: Centre of Learning

BEFORE VESALIUS wrote his great anatomy book, people thought the inside of the body looked like this. No wonder doctors had trouble deciding what was wrong with the sick!

THE MEDICAL SCHOOL in Padua is one of the first to be built in Europe.

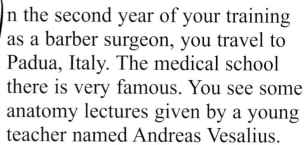

In the second year of your training as a barber surgeon, you travel to Padua, Italy. The medical school there is very famous. You see some anatomy lectures given by a young teacher named Andreas Vesalius. He is very popular, and everybody crushes into the dissection hall to watch what he does and listen to what he says.

Seeing a body being cut open and peeled apart piece by piece is both exciting and frightening. You have never seen anything like this in London. Vesalius has been working on his own book about anatomy, and you find a copy of it in the library. The drawings show what is inside the body in great detail. It looks so strange that you can hardly believe all of it is inside you.

Handy Hint

Get an artist with a strong stomach to make sketches of dissections. You don't want your artist to faint or get queasy halfway through and only draw part of the body.

VESALIUS starts a strong tradition of anatomy at Padua. Eventually a circular lecture theatre is built (below), specially designed to give everyone a good view.

And if we just peel this back, like so...

Blood, Glorious Blood!

What You Will Need

A MAP of the veins of the body, showing the best points to get blood.

barber surgeons believe illness is caused by 'badness' in the blood, and letting the 'badness' out of the body will cure the patient. One of their main treatments is called blood-letting. The barber surgeon uses special tools to cut open a vein and then catches the blood in a shallow bowl. If the patient is not very ill, losing a little blood probably does no harm. The problem is that barber surgeons don't know when to stop. Many patients die from the treatment after losing several pints of blood. A gentler method is to use blood-sucking worms called leeches.

SEVERAL KNIVES and puncture pins for cutting into different veins. These should all be sharpened regularly.

AT THE AGE OF FOURTEEN you have the terrifying experience of going to the Royal Court with your master to treat King Henry VIII. Despite treatments of bleeding, rest and herbal potions, Henry soon dies. You are sad that the old King is dead but glad that you don't have to go back there again!

When Humour Wasn't Funny

Alternative Cures

PUTTING A SOOTHING LOTION on the weapon that has wounded a soldier will cure that soldier instantly.

ASTROLOGY is widely used by Tudor doctors. They ask for a patient's birth sign and make a diagnosis according to the position of the stars.

ACCORDING to the Tudors, toads held next to a wart will cure the nasty hard lump of skin very quickly.

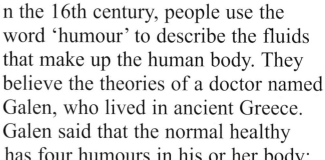

In the 16th century, people use the word 'humour' to describe the fluids that make up the human body. They believe the theories of a doctor named Galen, who lived in ancient Greece. Galen said that the normal healthy person has four humours in his or her body: blood, phlegm, black bile and yellow bile. Blood is hot and wet; phlegm is cold and wet; black bile is cold and dry; and yellow bile is hot and dry. According to Galen, when all four humours are present in equal amounts, the body is healthy. When they are out of balance, a person becomes ill.

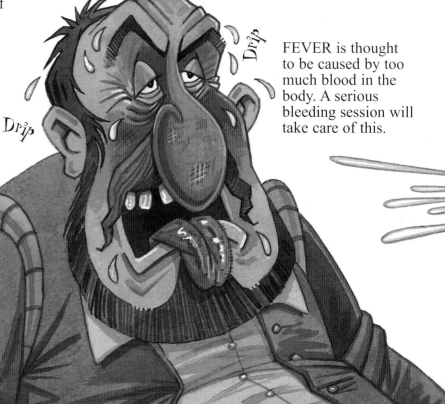

Croak

Drip

Drip

FEVER is thought to be caused by too much blood in the body. A serious bleeding session will take care of this.

A DRY, HACKING COUGH with a fever is caused by too much yellow bile in the body.

Handy Hint

Bad-tempered patients often have too much hot blood. Give them regular blood-lettings to calm them down.

SADNESS AND DEPRESSION are caused by an excess of black bile.

COLDS occur when you have too much phlegm in your body.

15

Battlefield Horrors

One of the worst places to be in the 16th century is in the middle of a war. In 1563, you are officially made a barber surgeon in an army fighting in northern France. Soldiers face guns and muskets as well as swords, arrows, pikes and axes. The injuries suffered are horrendous, and barber surgeons like you can do very little to help. Conditions are filthy, and there are no antiseptics. Limbs damaged in battle usually become infected and have to be amputated. Several people have to hold the soldier down during surgery. Even though he is given a whack on the head with the surgeon's mallet to knock him out, he will suffer tremendous pain. Few survive long after this dreadful ordeal.

AMPUTATION SAWS look elegant but may not be all that good at amputating limbs. Instruments are not washed between operations, and they are often dropped in the mud.

BARBER SURGEONS study battlefield wounds and draw diagrams to show possible injuries (right).

Plagued by Infections

Other Nasty Diseases

ST. VITUS'S DANCE is a disease caused by a bacterial infection. It causes people to jerk and move uncontrollably, as if they are trying to do a wild dance.

The Black Death, the largest-ever outbreak of the plague, happened in the mid-1300s. It killed much of the population of Europe and then returned again and again. There is yet another bad outbreak in 1563, and many people leave London. Even Queen Elizabeth I flees to Windsor Castle with her household. To prevent the infection from reaching her, she orders that anyone arriving at Windsor from London is to be hanged.

LEPROSY is common. This disease eats away at skin and muscle. Because leprosy is easy to spot, lepers are outcasts and are forced to live away from other people.

SCROFULA is a form of tuberculosis. It can be cured, so it is said, by touching royalty. Touching a coin that the monarch has touched is also thought to work.

POP

There is little that you can do for somebody with either the spitting plague or the bubonic plague. Spitting plague makes you cough and spit blood, and finishes you off in about three days. Bubonic plague causes huge boil-like lumps called buboes to erupt all over your body. Many die from it in about five days, but if you are still alive after that, you could recover.

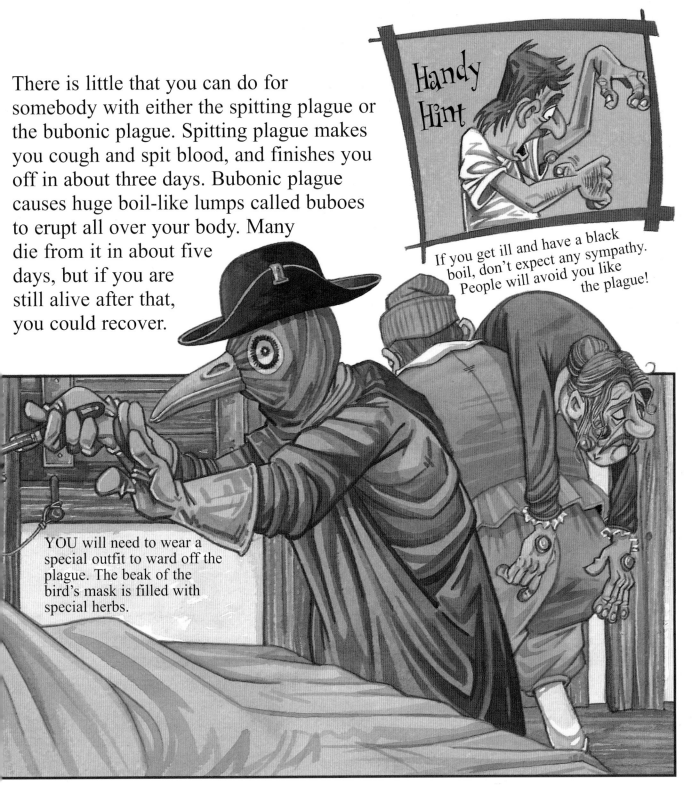

Handy Hint

If you get ill and have a black boil, don't expect any sympathy. People will avoid you like the plague!

YOU will need to wear a special outfit to ward off the plague. The beak of the bird's mask is filled with special herbs.

19

Hospital Surgery

After your time with the army, you return to England and take a position at St Bartholomew's hospital in London. Most 16th-century hospitals are places of fear. Although most patients are poor, they are forced to pay the hospital their funeral expenses before they are allowed in. The latest techniques are practised at St Bartholomew's: nose jobs, tooth extractions and cataract operations. Aristocratic soldiers who return from battle with injuries can get false limbs or a false nose made of gold. Some nobles have their noses altered to improve their appearance. This is an early form of plastic surgery.

TREPANNING is carried out by barber surgeons. If you keep getting headaches, you might have a hole drilled into your skull to let the 'badness' out.

False Limbs

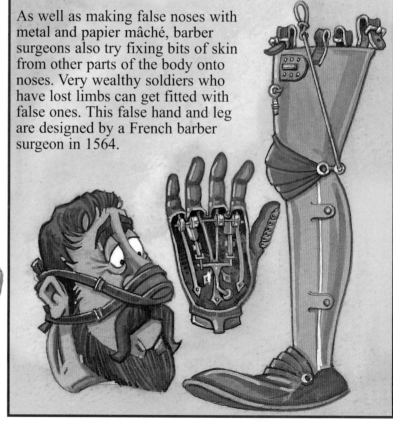

As well as making false noses with metal and papier mâché, barber surgeons also try fixing bits of skin from other parts of the body onto noses. Very wealthy soldiers who have lost limbs can get fitted with false ones. This false hand and leg are designed by a French barber surgeon in 1564.

Quacks and Witches

The well-off in Tudor times can afford the services of a physician or a barber surgeon, but most people are too poor. Qualified doctors are also in short supply. This leaves opportunities for quacks – people who sell all sorts of potions and liquors that are supposed to cure everything. Some of them sell their cure-alls at fairs and by the side of the road, and many people are taken in and buy them by the bottle. Barber surgeons hate quacks, but the sad truth is that the barber surgeon's medicines and potions are just as likely to fail. Nobody really has the knowledge to treat many illnesses.

Bottles of potion

Accused of Witchcraft?

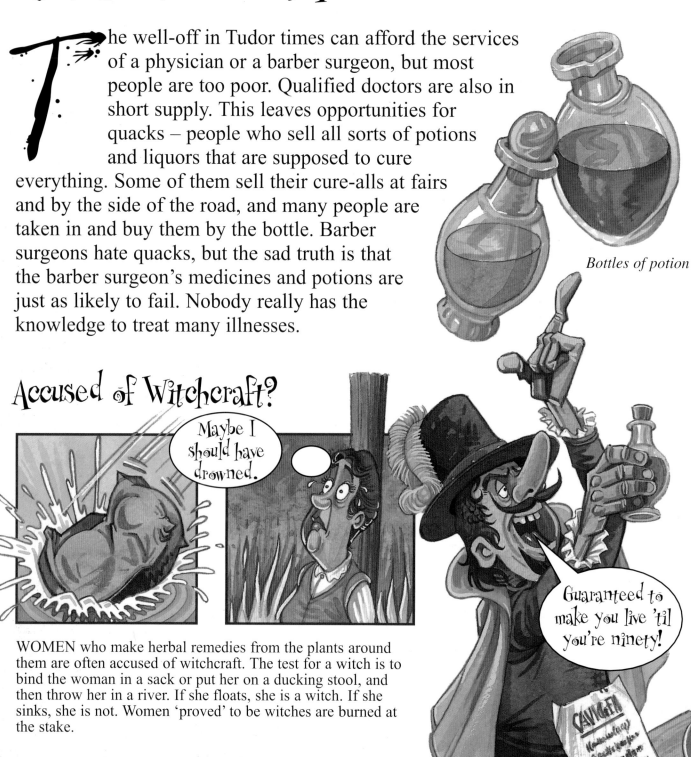

Maybe I should have drowned.

Guaranteed to make you live 'til you're ninety!

WOMEN who make herbal remedies from the plants around them are often accused of witchcraft. The test for a witch is to bind the woman in a sack or put her on a ducking stool, and then throw her in a river. If she floats, she is a witch. If she sinks, she is not. Women 'proved' to be witches are burned at the stake.

Herbs and the Apothecary

JOHN GERARD grows his own herbs and writes a famous book on herbalism. Several other herbalists publish books during the 1500s.

Apothecaries and herbalists are becoming very important, and you work with several of them. You meet John Gerard, one of the greatest herbalists of the time. He is himself a surgeon, and he has travelled widely. He grows more than a thousand plants to treat his patients. Gerard will publish his own guide to herbal medicine in 1597.

Gerard boils different herbs in oil and extracts their essence. He rubs these highly fragrant oils into his patients' skin. You often ask him to make up herbal treatments. One of them, willow bark, is used as a treatment for pain. Willow bark contains a very potent ingredient that actually does dull pain.

Barbaric Births

What You Might Need

A BIRTHING CHAIR has a large hole in the seat for the baby to pass through. The long skirts of the mother are draped around the chair for modesty.

FORCEPS can pull a baby out, but in unskilled hands they can cause severe injuries, so be careful!

You might not want to be ill in the 16th century, but it can be even worse to be a woman. Girls marry at very young ages – twelve or thirteen – and then have children constantly. Childbirth is dangerous. Many women die in labour or after birth because of infection. Many babies also die.

AAARGGHH!

Only noblewomen are attended by a barber surgeon. If things go wrong, you could use forceps to pull the baby out. Your knowledge of anatomy also allows you to carry out a cesarean – an operation to remove a baby through its mother's abdomen.

Handy Hint

Tell all your pregnant patients that they should make arrangements for the baby's birth – and for its funeral, just in case.

Perhaps it's time to use the knife.

Congratulations!

MIDWIVES attend women giving birth and take care of them afterwards. They aren't trained, but they learn from other midwives and generally do a good job.

At War Again: The Armada

Between 1577 and 1580, you are the barber surgeon on the *Golden Hind*, the ship captained by Sir Francis Drake. Sailors are often ill. They are always wet, and they barely sleep on the boards below deck. Their diet of salt pork, beef, cheese, dried fish and biscuits gives them scurvy.

In 1588 you are barber surgeon on Drake's ship during the Spanish Armada. On 21 July Drake attacks the Armada near Plymouth. The Armada is beaten, but the cost to the sailors is high. Many suffer terrible injuries after being shot, or trapped behind cannons.

Scurvy

Scurvy is caused by not eating enough vitamin C, but doctors don't yet know that. You find that some herbs help, particularly when eaten fresh.

End of an Era

After the success of the Armada, Queen Elizabeth I recognises your bravery. She makes you one of her personal physicians for the last five years of her life. This is not always a pleasant experience – she becomes bad-tempered and bitter as she gets older. In February 1603, you are called to her. She has been walking in the cold air and has caught a chill. For two weeks you go to her every day, advising rest and giving hot infusions of different herbs.

ARCHBISHOP WHITGIFT, the Archbishop of Canterbury, is the only man whom Queen Elizabeth I wants with her as she is dying. Her doctors are all turned away.

Go away – you can do nothing for me now.

In mid-March, however, the queen decides never to see any of her doctors again. She lies on cushions, hardly eating or drinking. You call for another week but are refused an audience. Elizabeth falls into a deep sleep, and on the morning of 24th March 1603, she dies. The Tudor age has ended.

Handy Hint

A new fashion for smoking has just begun. Avoid this at all costs, as it is particularly bad for your health.

YOU TEACH a group of apprentices during the last fifteen years of your career, just as your master did fifty years ago. You die at the age of seventy-two, a grand old age for someone who has spent his life mixing with the sick of the 16th century.

See what it says about an orangey colour.

31

You Wouldn't Want to Be a Pioneer of Electricity

Introduction

Your name is Michael Faraday. In your youth, electricity is not understood. People wonder why a comb picks up paper, or why lightning starts fires. They gasp when inventors show off machines that make sparks and give people shocks. Whatever makes the sparks is regarded as a mystery, but of no use to anyone – until you show how to make electricity and electrical machines. You flick the switch to turn on the modern world!

Can you imagine a world without electricity? No electric light at the flick of a switch, no power to heat our homes, cook our food, start our cars, or work our televisions and computers? That's what the world was like before Faraday made his discoveries.

What's the Attraction?

You are born on 22nd September 1791. You are the third child of James Faraday – a blacksmith who moves from the north of England to find work in London the year that you are born – and his wife Margaret. Your family are religious and go to chapel every Sunday. They are quite poor, but pay a few pennies a week to send you to school.

At 13, you have to start work. You get a job with a bookbinder near Oxford Street, in London. Your boss, George Riebau, often sends you on errands, which enables you to see the sights of the city. Mr Riebau soon realises you are clever. While you cheerfully glue covers onto books, you also read them. You love learning about science and inventions. You read about electricity in an encyclopedia and that really sparks your imagination!

Electric eel

Electric ray

Zap!

ELECTRIC FISH. Some fish are shocking! Electric rays and electric eels have special cells in their bodies. The cells produce electric shocks big enough to stun a smaller fish or scare off a larger enemy.

Read All About It

You regularly go to hear science talks. There you make friends with other young people who want to learn. Science is all the rage. One day, you are given tickets to lectures by Humphry Davy. Davy is the star scientist of the Royal Institution, a club for people interested in new ideas. His talks are full of 'special effects': model volcanoes, coloured smoke, and whiffs of 'laughing gas' (nitrous oxide) that make people fall over giggling. You make notes and drawings of the lectures and send them to Davy, asking for a job. In October 1812 Davy almost blows himself up doing an experiment! He needs an assistant.

IN MARY SHELLEY'S STORY *Frankenstein* (1818), a scientist uses electricity to bring a man-made monster to life. No wonder people are fascinated by tricks with wires and batteries!

NOTEBOOKS. You keep notes and drawings all your life. You think that experiments could answer most questions in science.

LUIGI GALVANI. In 1771 this Italian scientist observed a dead frog's leg twitch when touched by two different metals. Why? The answer was an electric current.

Here's the Science

Magnetic Poles

The Earth is a magnet. So are some metals. If a bar magnet is hung in the centre it will swing until one end points north. The ends, or poles, of a magnet are called North (N) and South (S).

Opposite poles, N and S, attract one another (2). Like (same) poles, N and N, S and S, repel, or push apart (1).

Hans Oersted

OERSTED'S NEEDLE. Hans Oersted was showing a class of students how electric current from a battery moved along a wire. A compass was lying on the bench close to the wire. Its needle flickered. This showed that an electric current produced a magnetic field.

Metal gauze

Wick

Davy lamp

In a Spin

You have other things on your mind, apart from magnets and batteries. In June 1821 you marry your sweetheart Sarah Barnard; you live in rooms in the Royal Institution.

You are asked to write a magazine article on what is known about 'electromagnetism,' and doing this gives you a new idea. You go back to the laboratory in September 1821 and carefully put together your electrical apparatus: corks, wires, glass jars, mercury, magnets and Volta-type batteries. You explain, to Sarah and your nephew George, that you are sure an electric current could make a magnetised wire spin. You connect all your bits and pieces to a battery. And, presto! The wire spins around the magnet. You and George dance with glee around the world's first electric motor!

First electric motor

Movable magnet

Movable wire

Fixed magnet

Mercury

Battery

It works!

Warning!
NEVER touch liquid mercury – it is extremely toxic to the human nervous system, as well as to fish and animals.

THE FIRST ELECTRIC MOTOR. Two pots of mercury form part of the electrical circuit (left). In each pot is a magnet. When current from the battery passes around the circuit, the 'free' wire spins around the fixed magnet.

A SILLY QUARREL. Your discovery makes you famous and Humphry Davy becomes jealous. Davy spreads it around that you have stolen ideas from William Wollaston, another scientist. This is untrue.

Wired up

The quarrel with Davy upsets you and Davy goes on treating you like a servant. But you make friends with William Wollaston and receive letters of congratulation from Ampère and other scientists. Your family lives happily above the laboratory, from which loud bangs, crashes and flashes can be heard. One loud bang in 1823 signals another first: you have turned a gas (chlorine) into a liquid. You enjoy giving lectures at the Royal Institution, where people can exchange ideas.

'We light up the house,' you write cheerfully, in a letter. You are busy doing experiments with coils of wire and magnets. You read how William Sturgeon (in 1825) and American scientist Joseph Henry (in 1829) make electromagnets that can lift heavy weights of iron.

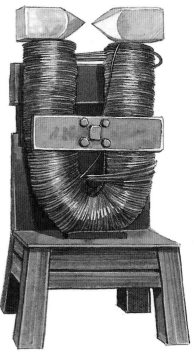

ELECTROMAGNETIC CHAIR. You make electromagnets by winding a long piece of wire around a U-shaped iron bar. This one is so heavy, you set it on a chair (above). When the wires are connected to a battery, the iron bar becomes a magnet.

ELECTROMAGNETS AT WORK. Electromagnets are useful in modern scrapyards. They are hung from the chain of a crane.

When the current is turned on, the electromagnet starts to work. Big ones can pick up whole cars. Anything with iron in it is attracted!

DAZZLING DISPLAYS. Your Christmas lectures for children become an annual event. You love to dazzle your listeners with showers of sparks and glowing arc lamps. One day, children will see electric light in their homes.

Here's the Science

Electromagnet Coils

A current increases magnetism if the wire it flows along is bent into a loop.

Several loops make a coil. This makes the magnetic effect even stronger.

When a coil is wound around an iron rod and the coil is connected to a circuit, you have an electromagnet! No current means no magnetism.

Switched On

Your Christian religion is an important part of your life, and you think that everything in nature might be connected in unseen ways. Electricity can make magnetism. So can magnetism make an electric current? In August 1831 you prove it. You wind two long coils of wire onto opposite sides of an iron ring. Then you connect the wires to a compass needle. When you touch the ends of the wire to a battery, the needle flickers. The current seems to have 'jumped.' The magnetic field around the first coil has 'induced' (started) a current in the second coil. Electromagnetic induction is possible. By October, you go on to make a simple generator.

INDUCTION RING. You wind two coils of copper wire (over 120 feet, 36 m, in all) around an iron ring 6 inches (15 cm) in diameter. You use twine and calico as insulators. When the current is on, the needle flicks one way. When you switch the current off, the needle flicks back the other way!

STAYING LOYAL. In 1827 you are asked to become Professor of Chemistry at London's new university. You politely say no. You prefer to stay at the Royal Institution, which you say has been 'a source of knowledge and pleasure for 14 years'.

Here's the Science

How Induction Works

Battery

1st coil 2nd coil

Switch

Iron ring

Compass needle

Current flowing through the first coil sets up an electromagnetic field around it. The magnetism creates a short burst of current in the second coil, making the compass needle move. The same thing happens, in the opposite direction, when you turn off the current.

MOVING THE MAGNET. On 17 October 1831, you try slipping a bar magnet in and out of a coil. Again the compass needle moves! Motion and magnetism: you have found a better way to make, or generate, electricity.

Bar magnet

Compass needle

Coil

A Generator

Making electricity to drive machines requires energy, you realise. So you harness the muscle power of your assistant, Charles Anderson, to turn a wheel and belt machine. The machine makes a copper disc spin fast between the poles of a U-shaped magnet. You yell with delight when you see the needle move and then stay in its new position. This shows that current is flowing. Your spinning disc is a generator. As long as it keeps spinning between the poles of the magnet, it will make electricity – one day enough electricity to drive vehicles and factory machines. This is the start of something bigger than even you are aware of.

Charles Anderson

First in the Field

ou are never happier than in the laboratory. While working, you hop from one foot to the other, rubbing your hands and humming a tune. You are sure now that magnets, static charges and electric current all produce 'fields' of force. You study the patterns that iron filings make on a card when you place a magnet near them. In your mind, you see electromagnetic fields everywhere, invisible as the air in which birds fly and kites soar. The idea of 'force-fields' starts with you.

When you are not working, you enjoy spending time with your family and going on seaside holidays.

CHARLES ANDERSON is a retired army sergeant and an ideal assistant. He never complains, even when kept up all night just because you forget to tell him to go home!

YOU LOVE PLAYING with your nieces and nephews. To amuse them, you build a four-wheeled velocipede (a kind of bicycle) which you ride around London's Hampstead Heath.

Come and have a go on my velocipede. Pushing the pedals makes it go.

Velocipede

Here's the Science

Electromagnetic Field

(1)

Wire

Iron filings show the presence of a magnetic field. They lie scattered on a card (1) when no current flows through the wire.

(2)

When a current flows, the iron filings make a ring-shaped pattern (2). This shows where the electromagnetic field is.

Lighting Up

The generator that you create inspires other inventors to make larger ones, driven by steam engines. You have shown how an electric motor can work, but you leave others to make the first electric motors for machines. These will come in the 1870s, after your death.

You don't live to see electric light bulbs, either. You know how a light bulb might work – you have seen thin wires glowing bright and hot when electric current flows through them. You know, too, about arc lamps, invented in 1812, and the first electric lights. They give a brilliant spark of light, fine for theatres but too bright for reading at home. At night, you work by gaslight or lit candles. The first light bulbs that work without burning out or exploding will be invented in the 1870s, by Joseph Swan in Britain and by Thomas Edison in the USA.

Experimenting with an arc lamp

Here's the Science

How Does a Light Bulb Work?

Filament

Inside a glass light bulb is a thin wire called a filament, surrounded by gas. Thin wire has more resistance to the electrons in electricity than a thick wire. When current flows, the wire gets hot and glows, giving off light.

Filament

Wires carrying current to and from filament

Contact to power supply

YOU KEEP WRITING your notebooks, realising that your memory is fading as you grow older. You create some of the words we still use about electricity, including *anode*, *cathode* and *electrode*.

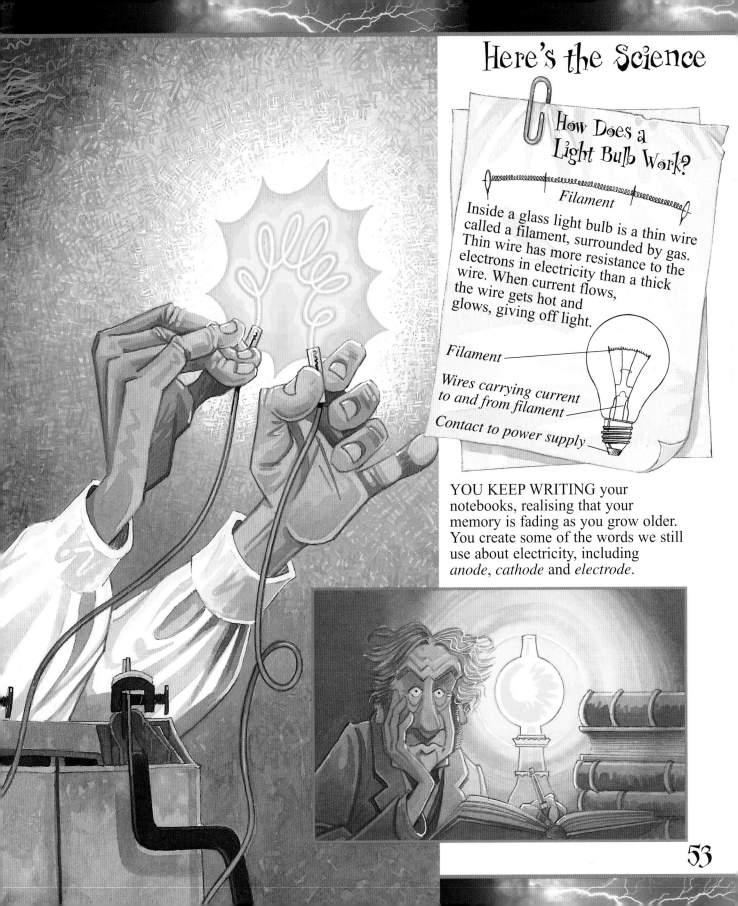

53

Shocking Discoveries

In 1839 you fall ill through overwork. When you eventually go back to your research, you try to use a giant magnet to bend light. You also try to use sunlight to make electricity. You do not succeed, but your sun-power idea will later be taken up to produce the photoelectric cell and solar power.

You go on testing conductors and insulators. Electricity is dangerous, and you give yourself many burns and electric shocks. You have to find out for yourself how to insulate your equipment to control the electric current safely. This means hours of work, carefully wrapping wires in cloth, twine, or some other material.

Leyden jar

CONDUCTORS. You do experiments with a Leyden jar to find the best conductors (carriers) of electricity. Silver is a good conductor, as is a carrot (being moist). Copper is cheap, so you use copper wire.

FEELING THE STRAIN.
You believe that energy is all around, streaming across the universe. You hope electricity will unlock the secrets of this universal energy. Sadly, your own energy is failing. You have worked too hard and fall ill. For six years you do little scientific work and are seldom seen in public.

Electric Current

Wire

Insulation

Battery disconnected

Electric current is a stream of electrons. Usually, electrons move in different directions. But when a battery is connected to a copper wire, it pushes all the electrons in the wire in the same direction. They flow along the wire as current. Insulation around the wire stops electrons from escaping.

Battery connected

Electron

INSULATORS.
To insulate wires, you wrap them in non-conducting material. You try leather, parchment, hair, twine, cloth, wood, even feathers. (Plastics are good insulators, but there are no plastics in your time.)

LECTURING AGAIN. By the 1850s Britain's most famous scientist is again busy giving lectures. You warn that not enough children are learning science.

DANGER! Do NOT play with electrical wiring!

CAUTION: Use only a small battery (1.5 volts) when doing simple experiments. Any voltage can and will cause burns to skin; a large voltage can cause death. Check with a teacher or other adult before working with any electrical current.

The Future, Thanks to Faraday

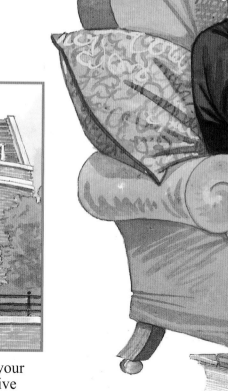

You are awarded many honours, but you prefer to stay plain 'Mr' Faraday, rather than 'Sir Michael'. You die on 25 August 1867. Within 15 years, Thomas Edison will light up the streets of New York City. You do not live to see any of the wonders that your work made possible, such as electric trains, computers or television. 'Let the imagination go,' you write in 1858, 'guiding it by judgement and principle, but holding it and directing it by experiment.' Great scientists, such as Ernest Rutherford and Albert Einstein, call you the great pioneer of electricity.

'What is the use of such knowledge?' a woman once asks you. 'Madam,' you reply, 'what is the use of a newborn child?'

ROYAL GIFT. Queen Victoria gives your family a house at Hampton Court to live in. You live there from 1858 until your death.

Here's the Science

From Power Station to Home

Transformers 'step up' electrical power from 22,000 volts to over 700,000 volts to send it along wires across the country.

Transformer

Other transformers lessen, or 'step down', the power for safe use in our homes (110 to 240 volts). We owe this system to Faraday and his coils of wire – the first transformers.

Technology we take for granted today, made possible through Faraday's work

You Wouldn't Want to Be a Pioneer of the Telephone

Introduction

Your name is Alexander Graham Bell and you will be remembered as the 'telephone man.' The idea is quite simple: change sounds into electrical signals, send them along a wire, and change them back to sounds again.

Other inventors have done this, but you are the first to turn the sound into spoken words rather than buzzes and clicks. You know a lot about sound because you are an expert in speech and hearing. The telephone (named from Greek words meaning 'far speaker') will make you rich, but you will still go on inventing. You want to help people communicate. Another great inventor, Thomas Edison, says you have 'brought the human family closer in touch'.

Can you think of a world without telephones? Not being able to call home to say you'll be late, no text messages, no long chats with friends? The telephone changed the way we live and work.

Sounds and Silence

You are born Alexander Bell (you add the 'Graham' later) on 3 March 1847, in Edinburgh, Scotland. Your father, Alexander Melville Bell, teaches students elocution, or how to speak correctly. Your mother, Eliza, is a painter who is deaf. As you ('Aleck') are growing up with your brothers Melville and Ted, people who need to send a message quickly use the electric telegraph. But the telegraph sends only coded clicks. No-one has ever heard the human voice recorded or sent long-distance through wires.

I wonder how the sound of the leaves reaches my ears?

Here's the Science

Sound Waves

High frequency
(ripples close together)

Low frequency
(ripples spread apart)

Sounds are produced when objects vibrate, or move rapidly back and forth. The number of times an object vibrates in a given period of time is called its frequency. Sounds travel through the air as waves. The greater the frequency of a sound wave, the higher the pitch.

Try It Yourself

WHAT MAKES NOISE?
You like music and play tunes on anything. You wonder why a comb and paper make a noise when you blow on them. Why do leaves rustle in the wind?

SOUND RULES. Hold down the short end of a ruler on the edge of a table. Now twang the end that hangs over. BOING! As the ruler vibrates up and down, it disturbs the air, and makes a sound. No air means no sound. This experiment would not work in space, because there is no air in space!

No Star Student

You don't go to school until you are 10 years old. Instead you read books, go bird-watching, and keep pet animals. 'My dream is to become a musician,' you once say. At the Royal High School, you are an average student, but you enjoy learning maths. Teachers think your brother 'Melly' is much more clever. But you spend time helping your father. Mr Bell has worked out a way of writing down sounds to teach deaf children how to speak, called 'Visual Speech'.

You leave school at 14 and spend a year with your grandfather in London. London is a very busy city. It is easy to get knocked over by messengers dashing along the streets from one office to another. Grandfather Bell also takes you to meet Professor Charles Wheatstone, the inventor of Britain's first electric telegraph.

Vocal Cords

Vocal cords

To talk, we use our tongue and vocal cords. As air is breathed out of our lungs, it passes through the vocal cords, causing elastic flaps to vibrate like stretched rubber bands, making sounds.

TALKING HEAD. You and your brothers build a 'talking machine' out of wood, rubber and sheep's bones. You get it to say 'Mama' when you blow into its mouth!

Everyone's in such a rush these days. The streets aren't safe!

TELEGRAPH TAPPING. The telegraph sends urgent messages over long distances by using electrical signals. A tap on the telegraph key opens and closes an electrical circuit, sending clicking sounds along the telegraph wire. Words tapped in coded clicks are heard and decoded at the other end of the wire.

A telegraph machine

63

The Young Teacher

At 15, you get your first job, as a teacher in Scotland. You also start to show people how 'Visual Speech' works. In 1866, you make up your mind to leave home and go south to England, taking a teaching job there. You are growing more and more curious about new ways to communicate. With a friend, you rig up a telegraph wire to send messages between your rooms. You already know a lot about sound: you have tried experiments with drumskins and tuning forks, to find new ways to teach deaf people. Now, by reading books, you find out more about electricity and how batteries, circuits and electromagnets work.

You are full of life and energy. But then two terrible blows strike your family. In 1867 your younger brother Ted dies of tuberculosis, and three years later your older brother Melly dies from the same lung disease. Your life changes from then on.

Say: 'biscuit!'

TALKING TERRIER. You try teaching a dog to speak. You get your terrier to growl the vowel sounds: 'ow ah ooh ga ma ma.' It sounds like 'How are you, Grand-mama?'

Here's the Science

Morse Code

Morse code was invented by Samuel Morse of the United States. It uses dots and dashes to represent long and short sounds. Each alphabet letter has its own dot-dash code, so words can be spelt out. Telegraph messages are sent in Morse code, with words spelt out by long or short 'clicks'.

Bell's name in Morse code.

B — · · ·
E ·
L · — · ·
L · — · ·

Try it Yourself

A String Phone

Metal can

1) Ask an adult to make a small hole in the bottom of two empty metal cans, using a hammer and nail.
2) Push string through the holes, and knot the ends so the string won't pull through.
3) Hold one can each. Make sure the string is pulled tight.
4) Speak into one can. Your friend will hear your voice by holding the other can to his ear.

Keep string tight.

The can captures the sounds of the speaker and vibrates, which in turn causes the string to vibrate. These vibrations travel along the string to the other can causing that can to vibrate, and finally causing the listener to hear the speaker's voice.

65

A New World

After your brothers die, Mr and Mrs Bell leave Britain for Canada, taking you with them. They settle in Ontario, but you get a job in the United States, at the School for the Deaf in Boston. You are a wonderful teacher to the children and encourage them to make any noises they can, just to feel the sounds.

In 1872, a great fire breaks out in Boston. A new electric fire alarm calls out the firefighters, but many buildings burn. You also meet Mabel Hubbard. She is 15 and has been deaf since the age of 5. Her father, Gardiner Hubbard, is a rich lawyer, interested in new inventions. You talk with him about experiments with tuning forks that vibrate when electric current flows through a circuit. A 'harmonic telegraph' using this idea might help deaf people.

Here's the Science

Tuning Fork

Vibrating outwards

Vibrating inwards

A tuning fork has two metal prongs. Striking the tuning fork with a rubber mallet causes it to vibrate. By placing the tuning fork in a bowl of water, waves can be seen. Many musicians use tuning forks to tune their instruments.

If only they could have been here sooner...

Try it Yourself

MAKE A SPEAKING TUBE. Find a long piece of plastic tube. Tape a plastic funnel to each end. Give one end to a friend. Put the funnel to your ear and you can hear your friend whisper from the next room. Why? Once inside the tube, sound waves have to travel down it because they can't escape into the air.

Warning!
Don't shout! You might damage your hearing.

67

Twanging Springs!

By 1873, you are a professor at Boston University, working on the 'harmonic telegraph' in your spare time. Charles Williams is the owner of an electrical workshop who knows almost everything that has been discovered about electricity. He tells you that Thomas Watson would make a good assistant if you need one.

Your work with tuning forks gives you the idea for a telegraph that can send 12 messages at once, maybe more, by using different 'musical' sounds. In June 1875, you and Watson are testing the wired-up equipment, each in your own room. A metal spring gets stuck and Watson plucks it, to make it vibrate properly. You excitedly run in from next door. 'What did you do just then?' you shout. Through the wire, you had heard a faint sound – a twanging spring.

Twang!

KEEP AT IT. Joseph Henry (1797–1878) is America's most famous electrical scientist. He encourages you to keep going with your experiments.

Here's the Science

Twanging Spring

Magnetised strip

Stronger current — *Circuit* — *Weaker current*

A magnetised metal strip put near a wire coil makes a small electric current in the wire. If the strip vibrates, the current 'flickers,' first weaker then stronger. Watson's twanging spring had made a tiny electric current. It flowed along the wire into your room and made a 'twang' there too.

SPOOKY NAME. A thin skin (like a drumskin) vibrates at the slightest touch. In 1875, you and Watson make this 'gallows-frame' transmitter (right) with an electromagnet (a coil and magnet) and a thin skin (a diaphragm). The skin vibrates, making sounds that the electromagnet turns into tiny electric signals.

Battery

Electromagnet

Diaphragm

The 'gallows-frame' transmitter

Mr Watson!

You and Watson can now send sounds, such as hisses and clicks, through wires, but not proper words yet. You keep trying new ways to make the sounds clearer. On 9 March 1876 Watson talks into the mouthpiece of your latest 'telephone'. But what comes out is still 'a confused muttering sound'.

You make some changes to your plans and Watson puts together the new apparatus. Under the mouthpiece is a diaphragm, fixed to a platinum needle. The needle touches the surface of a dish filled with water and sulphuric acid.

The next day, 10 March 1876, the two of you are working in different rooms, linked by wires. You say: 'Mr Watson, come here, I want you!' and Mr Watson comes running in. The telephone works!

Here's the Science

Variable Current

This is what your drawing looks like. Your voice makes the diaphragm vibrate. The movements go through the needle and set up changes in the electrical resistance of the liquid. This sends an electric current (weak and strong by turns) flowing to the receiver, where a vibrating reed reproduces the voice sounds.

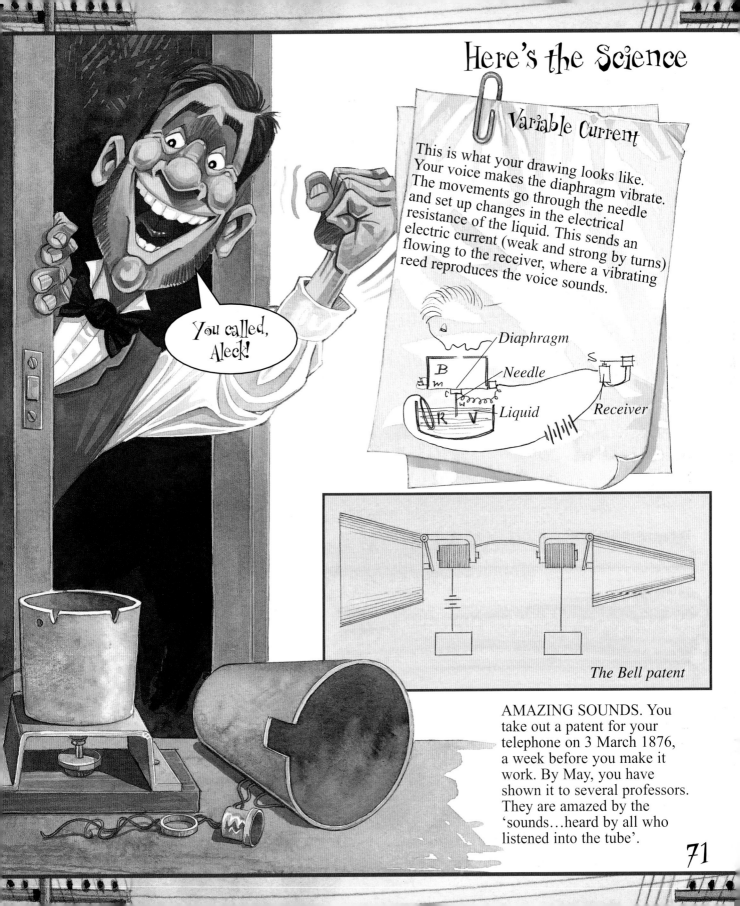

Diaphragm

Needle

Liquid

Receiver

The Bell patent

AMAZING SOUNDS. You take out a patent for your telephone on 3 March 1876, a week before you make it work. By May, you have shown it to several professors. They are amazed by the 'sounds…heard by all who listened into the tube'.

71

Talking to Anyone

In June 1876 you show off your telephone at the Centennial Exposition in Philadelphia, an exhibition to celebrate 100 years of the United States. Hearing someone's voice through a wire is a startling way to mark the event. People can hardly believe their ears! By October, you have tested your telephone over a 3-mile (5-km) line, and in May 1877 a burglar-alarm company begins putting the first phones into customers' homes.

In July that year, you and Mabel Hubbard are married. You go to Europe on your honeymoon and to Britain, where you show your phone to Queen Victoria. You try out improvements, adding cone-shapes for the mouthpiece and earpiece. People with poor hearing use a cone-like 'ear trumpet' to aid them, because a cone's funnel-shape helps to trap sound.

A ROYAL AUDIENCE. While on your honeymoon in Britain, you show your telephone to Queen Victoria (right). She is very impressed with the new invention. She wants to connect all her different castles by telephone!

My God, it talks!

HAMLET ON THE PHONE. At the Centennial Exposition, you demonstrate your new telephone to Emperor Dom Pedro II of Brazil. You read one of Hamlet's speeches from Shakespeare's play to the emperor, who is astounded.

Here's the Science

Catching the Sound

Megaphone

Sound waves

Ear trumpet

The cone shape of a megaphone or bullhorn stops sound waves from spreading out too quickly, so they travel further. The cone of an ear trumpet (an old-fashioned hearing aid) acts like a net to catch sound waves and funnel the sound to the ear.

Which end do I speak into?

Try it Yourself

1) To make a megaphone, fold a square sheet of paper into a triangle, as shown.

2) Roll the paper triangle into a cone shape. Stick the edges together with tape.

3) Cut off the narrow end of the cone, to make a mouthpiece. Call to a friend. Is your voice louder?

Warning!
Ask an adult to help you use the scissors.

73

Wires Everywhere!

You set up your own telephone company in 1877. But you have a rival, the American Elisha Gray, who patented his telephone just hours after you.

One hundred telephones are sold in 1877. Within 18 months, there are 1,700 in use. At first, each phone is wired directly to another one, but in 1878 the first 'telephone exchange' opens in Connecticut. The first 'operators' to 'exchange' or 'switch' calls between phone lines are Emma and Stella Nutt. Their first phone book has 50 names, but no numbers. London has its first exchange in 1879 – with only eight phones connected to it!

North America has more than 130,000 phones by 1881. City streets are festooned with telephone wires, strung from poles. Other companies set up telephone services too, sending workers racing around to string up wires. Some customers complain that rival wires have cut off their phone calls! You try not to let business, or your two daughters, take your mind off inventing. In 1882 you invent a machine for recording sounds. You call it the graphophone – an improvement on Edison's phonograph.

JUST IN TIME. You might not have submitted your patent before Elisha Gray without the help of Lewis Latimer. Latimer works through the night to draw the patent design. He later works with Thomas Edison inventing filaments, the glowing wires inside light bulbs.

Lewis Latimer

Here's the Science

How a Modern Exchange Works

The first telephone exchanges needed people to plug wires in and out of switchboards. Today, calls are sent digitally. A multiplexer changes the sound signals into electronic digital signals, and a de-multiplexer turns them back into sounds again. Thousands of calls whizz along every second.

Sound signal

Line multiplexer

Coded digital signals

De-multiplexer

SOUNDS BETTER. With the prize money you win for your telephone invention, you set up a research laboratory where you and your team invent the graphophone. It records sounds onto a spinning wax-covered drum. To play back, a stylus (needle) retraces the marks on the wax.

Stylus   Wax

The graphophone

Look, the whole city's connected!

Number, Please

You have to spend time and money in the law courts to settle a patent dispute with Elisha Gray. Gray had worked on the 'liquid transmitter' idea before you, but in the end, you win the case.

Americans like the telephone. It is the fastest way to keep in touch and do business: a letter takes days to cross the country by steam train and horse. By 1880, there are 30,000 phones in the United States. Four years later, the first long-distance phone call is made, between Boston and New York. But there are problems. Calls can 'jump' from one wire to another, and some people's phones are affected by the new electric lights. A funeral director named Almon Strowger is so annoyed when a rival firm keeps getting his calls that in 1890 he invents an automatic switchboard. He builds the wiring inside a wooden coffin!

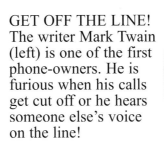

GET OFF THE LINE!
The writer Mark Twain (left) is one of the first phone-owners. He is furious when his calls get cut off or he hears someone else's voice on the line!

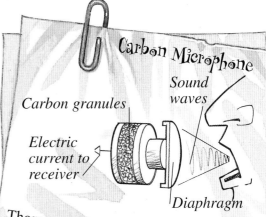

Carbon Microphone

Sound waves

Carbon granules

Electric current to receiver

Diaphragm

Thomas Edison puts a carbon microphone in his phone. The diaphragm inside vibrates as he speaks, making tiny carbon granules jump about. The carbon's electrical resistance changes, causing a changing electrical current along the phone wire. This makes speech sound more lifelike.

A BELL PHONE of the 1880s looks like the diagram below. Inside the rubber case is an electromagnet. Speaking makes a diaphragm vibrate, which sets up an electrical signal in the coil. The signal goes along wires to the receiver. Here it sets up vibrations in another diaphragm and reproduces the words spoken.

ELECTRICAL WHIZZ. Edison (right) invents the carbon microphone in 1877 and the phonograph, his recording machine, in 1878. Although Edison sells his telephone to your rival, Western Union, you still become friends.

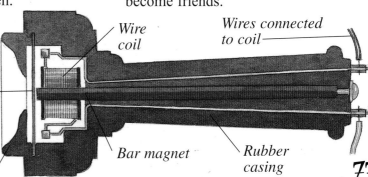

Wire coil

Wires connected to coil

Soft iron diaphragm

Mouthpiece

Bar magnet

Rubber casing

The Telephone Age

The telephone is improving all the time. New phones have both transmitter and receiver in one handset. Copper wires prove much better than the iron wiring first used (copper is a better electrical conductor). Underground cables mean fewer wires strung across streets. Signal-boosting makes really long-distance calls possible – in 1892 you make the first call from New York to Chicago. By 1907 there are over six million phones in America. A new phone with direct-dial numbers offers a privacy service. Before that, all calls went through an operator, who could listen in.

As the telephone becomes part of everyday life, you keep busy with new ideas and interests, such as America's National Geographical Society and your work to help deaf people, such as Helen Keller (see opposite).

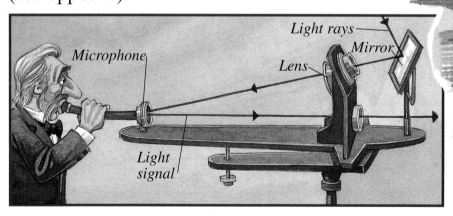

THE 'PHOTOPHONE.' One of your new ideas is to try and send the human voice using light instead of wires. Your photophone works by projecting the voice through an instrument toward a mirror. Vibrations caused in the mirror make light reflect differently and these fluctuating light signals can be turned back into sound by a light receiver some distance away.

Here's the Science

Fibre Optics

Transmitter

Signals travel as coded pulses

Receiver

Fibre-optic cable in sheath

Modern fibre optics work by light rays being reflected off the inside of a hair-thin glass or plastic tube. The light zigzags along inside. Bundles of fibres in a cable carry huge amounts of coded signals, at amazing speed. A fibre-optic cable can carry thousands more telephone calls than an old-fashioned metal wire.

Hello, Chicago, can you hear me?

A REMARKABLE PERSON. Helen Keller (1889–1968) is left deaf and blind after an illness at the age of 19 months. You suggest Helen visit a teacher from Boston, Anne Sullivan. She teaches Helen to communicate using 'hand-spelling' and the Braille 'raised dot' alphabet. You and Helen become good friends.

79

Never Still

Your summer home is at *Beinn Bhreagh*, or 'beautiful mountain' in Gaelic (an ancient language used in Ireland and Scotland). The big house in Nova Scotia becomes a place for fun and research for your family. Your wife Mabel gives up trying to stop you from working. You are too full of ideas, many of which you like to try out on your family – such as odd-shaped kites and pyramid-shaped engineering structures. Although you once say 'I somehow or other appear to be more interested in things than people,' you love your family and playing with your nine grandchildren. You give money away generously to fund laboratories, prizes, scholarships, and schools for the deaf.

An early dial telephone

DIAL A NUMBER.
While you busy yourself with your many interests, the phone business keeps on the move too. Small companies sell new phones, like this early dial phone.

Both you and your wife are fascinated by flight (the Bell company later builds planes and helicopters). You also take an interest in hydrofoil craft for high-speed water travel.

You see! I told you it would fly!

WATER SKIMMER. You call your hydrofoil boats 'hydro-dromes.' In 1918, your HD-4 craft sets a hydrofoil world speed record of 71 mph (114 kph) – a record not broken until 1963.

Communications Revolutionary

You die on 2 August 1922, at the age of 75, honoured as the inventor who made 'calling someone' part of everyday life. At the start of your funeral, every phone in North America is silent for one minute. In just a few years, you saw your telephone change the way people kept in touch and did business. Five years after you died, the first telephone call across the Atlantic Ocean was made, by cable.

Since your time, telephone technology has moved on rapidly. Thanks to fibre optics, computer modems, mobile phones and communications satellites, a phone lets us talk, text or send information from almost any spot on the planet. You expected life to go on changing. 'Education is a lifelong affair,' you told a young reporter the year before your death.

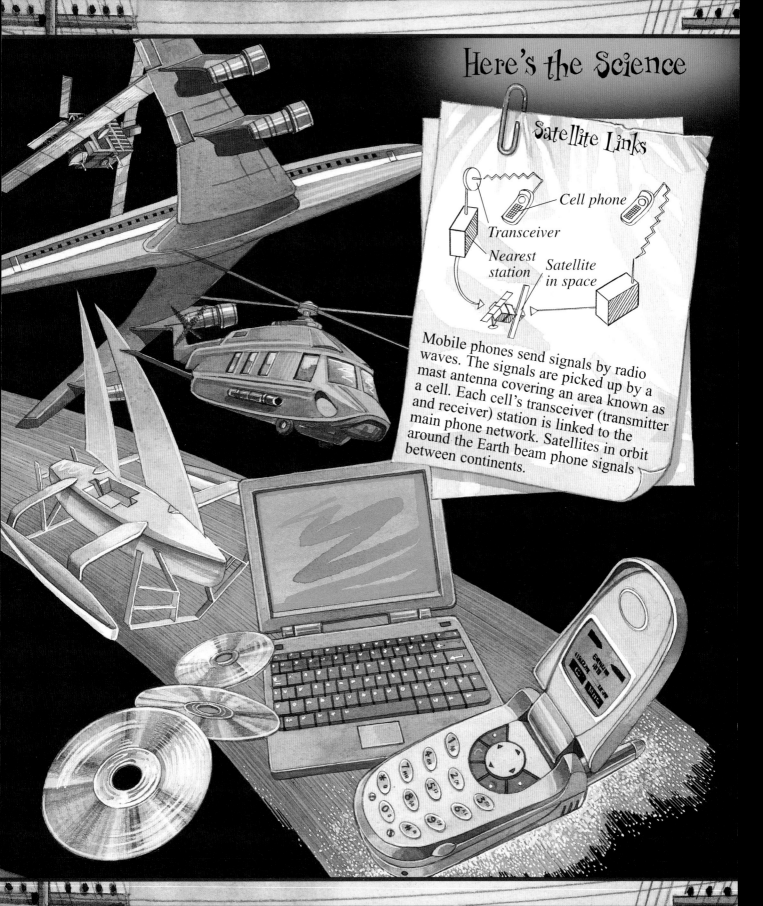

Satellite Links

Cell phone

Transceiver

Nearest station

Satellite in space

Mobile phones send signals by radio waves. The signals are picked up by a mast antenna covering an area known as a cell. Each cell's transceiver (transmitter and receiver) station is linked to the main phone network. Satellites in orbit around the Earth beam phone signals between continents.

You Wouldn't Want to Be a Pioneer of Radioactivity

Introduction

On 7 November 1867, you, Marya Sklodowska, are born in Warsaw, Poland, which is ruled by Russia at this time. When the Russian authorities ban laboratory studies in Warsaw's schools, your father, a teacher, keeps his laboratory equipment at home. You develop an early interest in science.

Later, having married and moved to Paris, you change your name to Marie to fit into French society. As Marie Curie, you will become one of the world's most famous and important scientists. Your trailblazing discoveries would have been outstanding at any time, but you make them at a time when women very rarely study science to an advanced level. You receive many awards and honours which had never been given to a woman before. You overcome enormous difficulties to do the work that is most important to you. You could make a great deal of money from the fruits of your work, but you prefer to make your discoveries freely available for the good of science. You discover new materials that behave in strange ways. By studying them, you open up a completely new branch of science that leads to nuclear power stations, radiation treatments for cancer, and a huge advance in our understanding of atoms.

A Polish Girl

As Marya Sklodowska, the girl who will become Marie Curie, you grow up with your father's laboratory equipment all around you. Perhaps it triggers your interest in science. You are a star pupil at school. When you leave you want to study medicine at a university, but it is not possible in Warsaw. You have to leave home.

In 1891, you move to Paris to study. You have a lot of catching up to do to match the other students. You work very hard and are awarded degrees in physics and mathematical sciences. Then you meet a scientist named Pierre Curie. You and Pierre are married within a year. You decide to study for another degree, a doctorate in science. It is something that no woman in Europe has ever done before!

Atoms

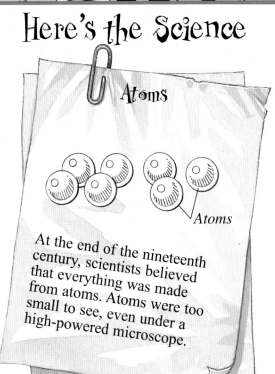

Atoms

At the end of the nineteenth century, scientists believed that everything was made from atoms. Atoms were too small to see, even under a high-powered microscope.

GOVERNESS. Before you can go to Paris to study, you earn money by teaching and working as a governess for wealthy families (above).

MARRIAGE. You and Pierre Curie are married in Paris on 26 July 1895. You spend the rest of the summer touring the countryside on your bicycles.

I understand what's happening now, Dad.

Invisible Rays

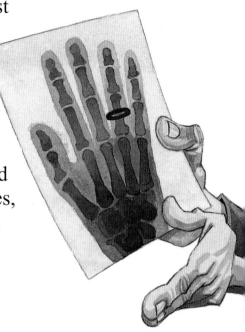

You have to decide what to study for your doctorate. Two recent discoveries interest you. Two scientists, Wilhelm Roentgen and Henri Becquerel, have discovered mysterious rays. Roentgen's rays will later be called X-rays. They can pass through someone and make a shadow-picture of their bones! Roentgen makes an X-ray photograph of his wife's hand. Becquerel discovers that a material called uranium gives out rays that darken photographic plates, too. Most scientists are more interested in X-rays, but you decide to study uranium rays. Your decision will change the history of science.

Becquerel's Uranium Rays

BECQUEREL PLACES a piece of uranium on top of a photographic plate wrapped in paper to keep light out. ('Plates' are used as an early kind of photographic film.)

AFTER SOME TIME, he unwraps the plate and, in darkness, processes it in a bath of chemicals.

WHEN HE HOLDS the plate up to the light, he can see a dark smudgelike picture in the middle where the uranium had been.

Look, darling, the magic of X-rays!

Rutherford's Atom

Some scientists thought atoms might be dotted with negatively charged particles called electrons.

Electrons

In 1907, experiments carried out by Ernest Rutherford showed that atoms might be made of a small, positively charged nucleus in the middle, surrounded by negatively charged electrons. The electrons flew around the nucleus.

Nucleus

LEAD UNDERWEAR. When people find out about X-rays, some of them are worried that an X-ray machine might be able to see through their clothes. A few actually wear lead underwear to block the rays!

Lead underwear

A Mystery Element

You wonder whether uranium is the only material that produces mysterious rays. To find out, you will have to test hundreds of different materials. You have a diligent work ethic, often neglecting food and sleep to carry on your experiments. Other scientists do tests by checking whether the materials darken photographic plates. You choose a different method that is faster and more accurate. You test each material by placing it inside an instrument called an electrometer, invented by your husband. Any rays it produces make it easier for electricity to flow through the instrument.

This one is very interesting, Marie!

The size of the electric current shows the strength of the rays. Most of the tests show no activity, but materials containing an element called thorium produce rays just like uranium. You invent a new word to describe the ray-making behavior of these materials – radioactivity.

Here's the Science

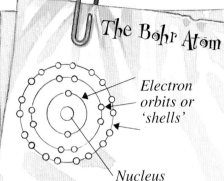

The Bohr Atom

Electron orbits or 'shells'

Nucleus

The Danish scientist Neils Bohr looked at Rutherford's idea of what an atom was like and improved it. He thought electrons might only be allowed at certain distances from the nucleus, like moons orbiting a planet, instead of swarming randomly around it.

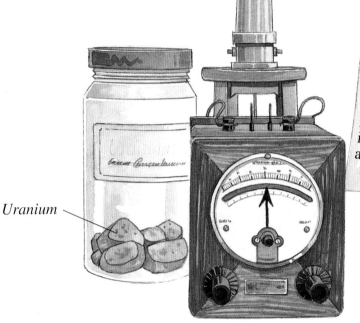

Uranium

PITCHBLENDE. One material that you test is pitchblende. It contains uranium, but it produces even stronger rays than uranium. There has to be something else in it making the rays. You find two new elements. You call one 'polonium'. after your native Poland, and the other 'radium'. from the Latin word *radius* meaning 'ray'. Rays are emitted by radium.

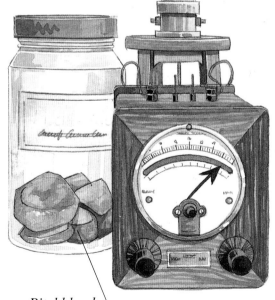

Pitchblende

A Witch's Brew

You and Pierre need a lot more radium, but pitchblende is too expensive for you to buy. Fortunately, the Austrian government, which has spare radioactive material, gives you a ton of spare radioactive pitchblende and later allows you to buy more pitchblende at a low price. You work in an old shed with a leaking roof – you have to be careful where you put equipment to avoid drips when it rains! You boil the pitchblende with acids and other chemicals to separate its radioactive part from the rest. The shed quickly fills up with smoke and fumes, so you work outside whenever possible. Many tons of pitchblende have to be processed to produce the very small quantity of radium you need to carry on your experiments.

There must be nearly an ounce of radium there!

Radioactive Decay

Nucleus

When you invent the word 'radioactivity' to describe the strange ray-making behaviour of radium, no-one really knows what it is. One idea is that it might be particles of energy flying out of the nucleus in the middle of an atom.

I wonder if Pierre wants to swap jobs for a while...

ENDLESS STIRRING. You stir your 'witch's brew' of smelly chemicals and pitchblende, while Pierre tests the different solids and liquids your work produces.

93

Getting to Know Radium

When you study radium, you find that its radiation is two million times stronger than that of uranium. It emits a radioactive gas, later called radon. It also gives off heat and glows in the dark brightly enough to read by. It can make nearby materials glow too. Diamonds glow brighter as they are exposed to increasingly larger amounts of radiation. It also darkens photographic plates, just like uranium. It changes the colour of the glass bottles it was put in, turning clear glass to violet. Radium also makes nearby materials radioactive, including your own clothes!

— *Radium*

HOT STUFF. Radium gives off so much heat that if it is dropped into some cold water, it can make the water boil (left)!

KEEPING WARM. Your shed is often freezing cold. Any heat, even from a tiny bottle of radium, is very welcome indeed!

The Radium Craze

When news of radium starts spreading, it fascinates everyone. Newspapers and magazines claim that the glowing liquid can treat pain, cure all sorts of diseases, make amazing machines work, or even destroy a whole city with its great power! Medicines containing radium are soon on sale to the public. It is several years before people find out how dangerous it is. Both you and Pierre have become ill during your work. You have lost weight and your fingers are sore from handling radium and other radioactive materials with your bare hands.

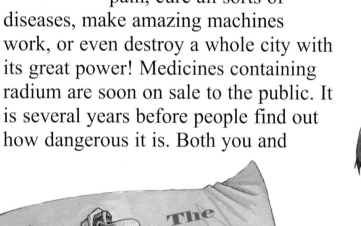

MIRACLE MEDICINE. People think radium is a miracle material that can cure illnesses. They are soon buying radium medicines.

You look radiant this evening!

RADIUM PARTIES. At parties, girls sometimes paint radium on their nails to make them glow in the dark! Sometimes they even mix radium with drinks to make them glow! They have no idea how dangerous the radiation from radium is and how it can harm them.

I've painted my toenails, too!

Here's the Science

Isotopes

Electron
Proton

Scientists discover that there are different forms of the same element, some heavier than others. These different forms are called 'isotopes.' There are three isotopes of hydrogen — with one, two, or three particles in its nucleus.

1 proton
1 neutron

1 proton
2 neutrons

DANGER! Girls who paint clock faces with radium often put the brush between their lips to form a point on it. When their teeth start falling out, doctors trace the problem to radium.

Blisters and Burns

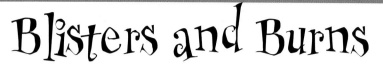

A few scientists have noticed that radioactive materials can be harmful. They can cause burns. When Henri Becquerel carries some radium in his pocket, it burns his side. You are also burned when carrying some radium, even though it is inside a metal box. Pierre studies radium's effect by carrying out a very dangerous experiment on himself. He puts some radium on his arm and then watches what it does to his skin! He wonders if radium's ability to kill cells might be used to treat some illnesses. If it can kill living cells, then it can kill diseased cells. Perhaps radium can treat cancer, a condition caused by cells multiplying out of control. When doctors try it, it works. Radiotherapy, as it becomes known, is still used today to treat some types of cancer.

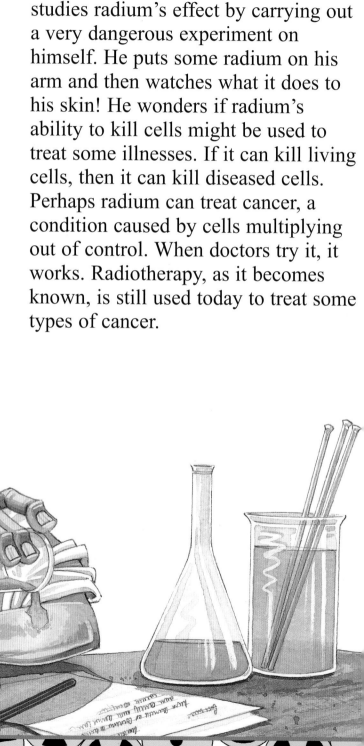

The things I do in the name of science!

SOON AFTER Pierre puts some radium on his arm, the skin starts turning red, like a burn, but it is not very painful.

THE REDNESS gets worse over the next few days. By the twentieth day, scabs have formed over the bright red skin.

IT CONTINUES getting worse and changes into an open wound. It is so bad that it has to be dressed with bandages.

FINALLY, new skin starts forming over the wound on day 42. Ten days later, it has healed, but it looks a strange grey colour.

Here's the Science

DNA Damage

The genetic code that controls all living cells is made from DNA. DNA is a long coiled-up string of particles. Radiation harms living cells because it knocks particles out of the DNA. This may kill the cells or just change the way they work.

Radiation

DNA strand

TREATING CANCER. Tiny glass tubes full of radioactive radon gas collected from radium are used to treat patients suffering from cancer. The radiation kills the cancer cells.

Spreading the Word

In 1903, you and Pierre are invited to London to speak about your work to the Royal Institution, a very important organisation of the most famous British scientists. At this time, women are not allowed to speak at the Royal Institution. Pierre has to give the talk while you look on. In fact, you are the first woman ever to be allowed into a meeting there at all! Pierre explains everything that you have found out about radium. He has brought some radium with him and uses it to show its strange effects. Reports of the talk make the two of you famous all over Britain.

At the end of 1903, you, your husband and Henri Becquerel are awarded the Nobel Prize for Physics, one of the world's most important science awards. Sadly, you are too ill to make the 48-hour journey to Stockholm to collect the award from the King of Sweden. Many more honours and awards follow.

PIERRE FALLS ILL. Before his talk at the Royal Institution, Pierre is so ill from radioactive poisoning that he is hardly able to dress himself. During the talk, his fingers are so sore that he spills some of the precious radium in the hall.

DAVY MEDAL. The many awards given to you for your work include the Royal Society's Davy Medal. It is only given for the most important discoveries in the world of chemistry.

The Davy Medal

So much money just wasted!

Transmutation

Protactinium 234
$^{234}_{91}Pa$ *

Beta particle emitted

β

Uranium 234
$^{234}_{92}U$

a

Thorium 230
$^{230}_{90}Th$

a

Radium 226
$^{226}_{88}Ra$

a

Radon 222
$^{222}_{86}Rn$

Alpha particle emitted

When an atom decays, the number and types of particles in its nucleus change. The atom changes from one element to another, during the process called transmutation. Radium is produced by the decay of other elements.

* This way of writing an element identifies which isotope it is.

INVITATIONS. You and Pierre are invited to dine with important and wealthy people. You often wonder how much equipment you could buy for your laboratory with all the fine jewellery the guests wear.

Tragedy!

On 19 April 1906, tragedy strikes. Pierre is run over by a horse-drawn wagon as he crosses the road. He is killed instantly. You are heartbroken. Pierre was a professor at the Sorbonne, part of the University of Paris. The Sorbonne asks you if you will take his place. You accept, and so become the first woman ever to work as a professor at the Sorbonne. Then the University of Paris and the Pasteur Institute agree to work together to build a new Radium Institute. It is to contain a radioactivity laboratory, headed by you.

You and Pierre were awarded your first Nobel Prize for your work on radioactivity. In 1911 you are awarded an amazing second Nobel Prize, this time for chemistry. It is given to you for your discovery of radium and polonium.

Whooooooa, boys!

Here's the Science

Measuring Radiation

To measure things, there have to be units, such as metres and kilograms. New units are now needed to measure radioactivity. You are given the honour of creating one of these new units. Scientists name it the 'curie' in your honour. One curie is the amount of a radioactive element in which there are 37 thousand million atomic disintegrations every second.

TEACHING. You and some of your friends teach classes for young children. Your daughter, Irene, and the other children are taught science by the world's leading expert on radioactivity!

103

The 'Little Curies'

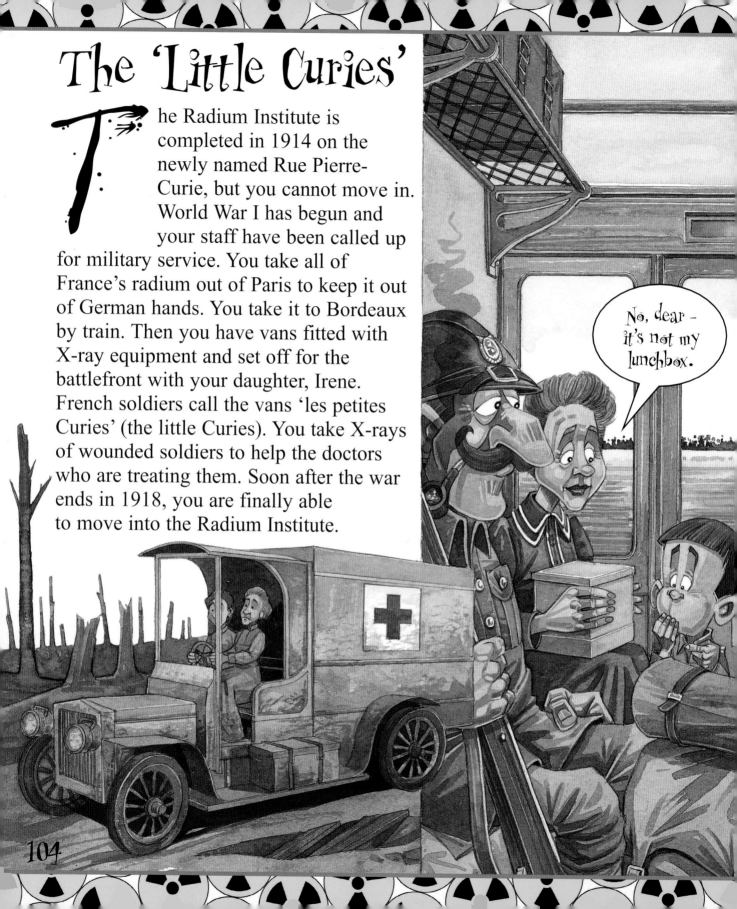

The Radium Institute is completed in 1914 on the newly named Rue Pierre-Curie, but you cannot move in. World War I has begun and your staff have been called up for military service. You take all of France's radium out of Paris to keep it out of German hands. You take it to Bordeaux by train. Then you have vans fitted with X-ray equipment and set off for the battlefront with your daughter, Irene. French soldiers call the vans 'les petites Curies' (the little Curies). You take X-rays of wounded soldiers to help the doctors who are treating them. Soon after the war ends in 1918, you are finally able to move into the Radium Institute.

No, dear – it's not my lunchbox.

Here's the Science

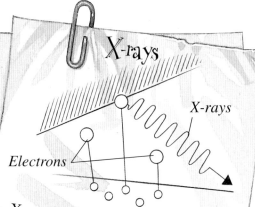

X-rays

Electrons

X-rays

X-rays are produced when very fast-moving electrons hit a hard material and stop suddenly. Their movement is instantly changed into energy waves, like radio waves but much shorter. The waves have so much energy that they can pass through some things, including people's bodies!

THE WAR EFFORT. The government asks people to give gold and silver for the war. You try to donate your medals, but officials refuse to take them.

Welcome to America

In May 1920, you give an interview to an American magazine editor, Mrs William Brown Meloney. When you tell her how badly you need more radium, Mrs Meloney starts the Marie Curie Radium Campaign to get it for you. France offers you the Legion of Honour, the country's most important award, but you refuse to accept it. You want a better laboratory, not more awards. Although you hate publicity and crowds, you are persuaded to go on a tour of the United States in 1921. It is a great success. The president, Warren Harding, meets you and gives you more radium. Many other people offer help too. You return to Paris with radium, equipment and money. You make a second tour of the States in 1929 and meet the new president, Herbert Hoover. This tour raises enough money to set up a second Radium Institute in Warsaw headed by your sister, Bronya.

Vive la France!

ACHES AND PAINS. Within a few days of arriving in the US, you have to put your right arm in a sling, because your hand and arm are aching from shaking hands with so many people!

Half-Life

1,620 years   1,620 years

Some elements decay faster than others. The speed is given by an element's half-life – the time taken for half of it to decay. A half-life can be less than a second or thousands of years. One of radium's isotopes has a half-life of 1,620 years.

Welcome to America!

DEGREES. Universities and colleges all over the United States give you degrees to honour your work. When you are too ill to receive them in person, your daughters, Irene and Eve, accept them for you.

The End of the Story

Xour health has been worsening for years. You have painful burns on your hands. You feel tired and often suffer from fevers and chills. Your sight is failing too. You write your notes in huge letters and your daughters have to guide you around. After an operation on your eyes, you are able to work again and even drive a car. Thirty-five years of handling radioactive materials and breathing in radioactive gases without any protection, as well as exposure to X-rays during the war, has taken its toll. On some days, you are too ill to work.

Doctors are unable to find out what is wrong with you. They think your ill health might be caused by tuberculosis. Then blood tests show you are suffering from a blood disorder, but they do not know what it is. It is probably leukemia, a type of cancer that affects the blood, and it is probably caused by radiation.

You must rest more, Mother.

LEAD SCREENS. In 1925, the French Academy of Medicine advises everyone working with radium to have blood tests and use lead screens for safety. You insist that your students and staff take all safety measures, but you do not use them yourself.

Protective lead outfit for handling radioactive material

FINAL DAYS. In May 1934, you leave the laboratories of the Radium Institute for the last time. Your condition gradually worsens. Doctors are unable to do anything more for you. You die on 4 July 1934, with your daughter, Eve, by your bedside.

Here's the Science

The Effect on Life

Different types of radiation have different effects on living things, including people. So, knowing how much radiation there is does not tell you how much, or how little, it will affect living things. Being able to measure the real effects of radiation is very important when it comes to protecting people from it. For this, a unit called the 'sievert' was created.

REBURIAL. In 1995, you and Pierre are reburied in the Panthéon in Paris, the burial place of France's most famous people.

You Wouldn't Want to Be a Pioneer of Flight

Introduction

irds fly; people don't. It has been like this for as long as anyone can remember. It is the way the world is meant to be, or so most people think. But there are a few who think it really might be possible to build flying machines that actually fly. Some people think they are mad. Others think that people are never meant to fly and it is dangerous to go against the 'natural order.'

Orville and Wilbur Wright

By the 1890s, hundreds of years of attempts to build heavier-than-air flying machines have all failed. At first, would be aviators try to copy nature. They hurl themselves off towers and hills wearing birdlike wings. Instead of gliding down gracefully, most of them crash to the ground in a tangled heap. For some, it is the last thing they ever do. It seems to be proof that humans are indeed never meant to fly. Then a handful of inventors finally begin to understand the science of flight. They try different shapes and sizes of wings and learn which is best. They build gliders that sail on the wind. Then you, Orville Wright, and your brother Wilbur decide to try your hand at building flying machines. You will change the course of history!

Wilbur will fall ill and die in 1912, aged just 45, but you live until 1948, witnessing the age of the jet plane.

Inspirations

In 1878, when you are seven years old and your brother Wilbur is 11, your father brings home a toy helicopter. Flying toys have been made for at least 500 years. You both enjoy flying your toy and even make your own copies of it. When you grow up you work in the family's bicycle shop in Dayton, Ohio. In the 1890s newspaper stories about gliders big enough to carry a person inspire you to study flight again. You read everything you can find about flying machines and decide to try building your own. When you begin, you think they probably won't be successful.

Toy helicopter like the one given to the Wright brothers

Flap Flap

ORVILLE WRIGHT. You were born on 19 August 1871, in Dayton, Ohio.

WILBUR WRIGHT. Wilbur was born on 16 April 1867, near Millville, Indiana.

GLIDING FLIGHTS. In 1896 you and your brother read about a German aviator, Otto Lilienthal, who is building his own gliders and flying them successfully.

Here's the Science

Why Can't We Fly?

Compared to birds, we are very heavy and have no wings or streamlined shape.

Wings and feathers

Strong chest muscles

Weak chest muscles

Heavy

Whoosh!

Creak

CONTROL. Pilots control their gliders by shifting their body weight. The Wright brothers think there must be a better way to do this.

YOU AND WILBUR have read about flying machines and built model aircraft since your childhood. Your father encourages you to solve any problems you have by looking for the answers in books.

FLAPPERS. Some people try to build full-size copies of ornithopters – flying toys with flapping wings (left). None of them work.

113

On a Wing and a Prayer

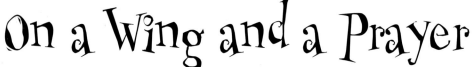

You and your brother, Wilbur, want to build a powered aeroplane, but you decide to build a glider before you tackle something with an engine. That means designing wings. But what shape should they be? And how big? You make models to try different shapes. Then in 1899 you build a much bigger model with a wingspan of 5 feet (1.5 m). You choose a biplane design – with two wings, one above the other. It isn't big enough to carry a person, but you can fly it as a kite.

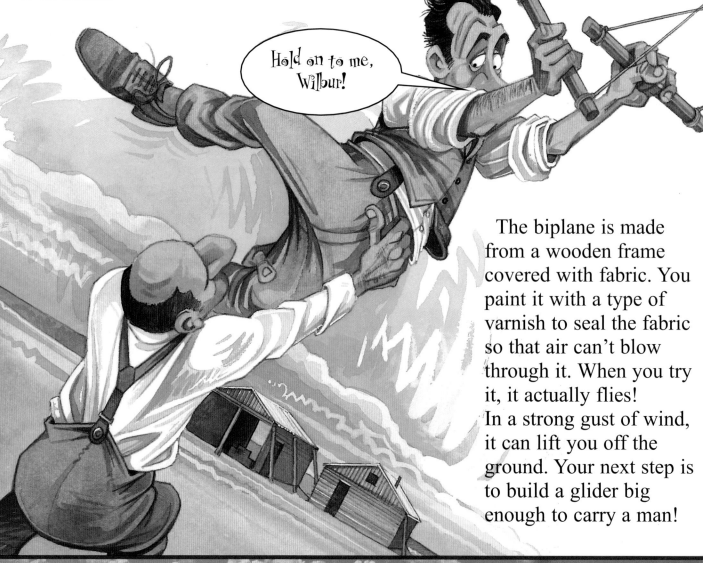

Hold on to me, Wilbur!

The biplane is made from a wooden frame covered with fabric. You paint it with a type of varnish to seal the fabric so that air can't blow through it. When you try it, it actually flies! In a strong gust of wind, it can lift you off the ground. Your next step is to build a glider big enough to carry a man!

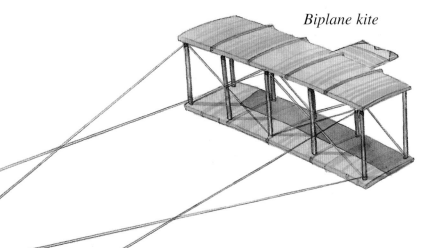

Biplane kite

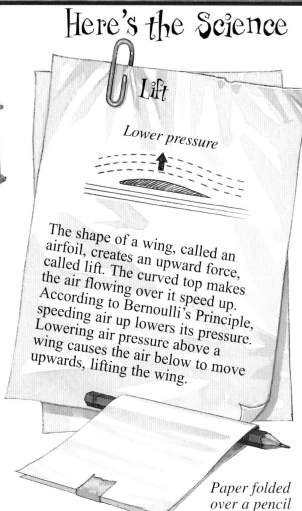

Lift

Lower pressure

The shape of a wing, called an airfoil, creates an upward force, called lift. The curved top makes the air flowing over it speed up. According to Bernoulli's Principle, speeding air up lowers its pressure. Lowering air pressure above a wing causes the air below to move upwards, lifting the wing.

Paper folded over a pencil

THE PERFECT PLACE. Your hometown isn't windy enough to test gliders. You ask the US Weather Bureau to help you find a windier place. You choose Kill Devil Hills, near Kitty Hawk, North Carolina.

Dayton

Kill Devil Hills

ATLANTIC OCEAN

PACIFIC OCEAN

Try it Yourself

Fold a sheet of paper over a pencil and stick the ends together. Hold the pencil level with your lower lip so that the wing hangs down. Blow down over the top of it. Blowing down makes it rise! Blowing lowers the air pressure over the wing and creates lift, pulling it upwards.

Do you think it's windy enough, Orville?

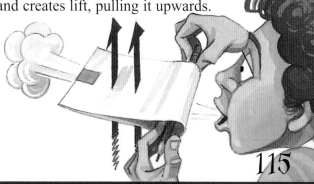

The First Gliders

The first full-size glider built by you and Wilbur has a wingspan of 17 feet (5.3 m). The pilot lies on the lower wing. He climbs or dives by tilting an 'elevator' at the front. The challenge is to balance the glider. If you don't balance a bicycle, it will crash, and the same is true of an aircraft. You and your brother develop a balancing system of pulling wires to twist the glider's wingtips. You call it 'wing warping'. Sadly, your glider doesn't fly very well and the next one you build is even worse! Your designs rely on research done by Otto Lilienthal. You wonder if he had got it wrong!

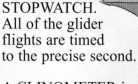
Stopwatch

STOPWATCH. All of the glider flights are timed to the precise second.

A CLINOMETER is used to measure how steeply each glider climbs or dives.

Clinometer

Wheeze!

ANEMOMETER. Wind speed is measured with an anemometer. Its propeller spins and a dial shows the speed.

Tape measure

Throb

PLAGUED BY MOSQUITOES. Living at Kill Devil Hills is no picnic! Mosquitoes swarm over the dunes – and over you and your brother! You write home, 'They chew us clear through our underwear and socks. Lumps begin swelling up all over my body like hen's eggs!'

TAPE MEASURE. You measure the lengths of all your flights with a tape measure.

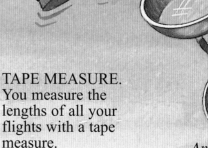
Anemometer

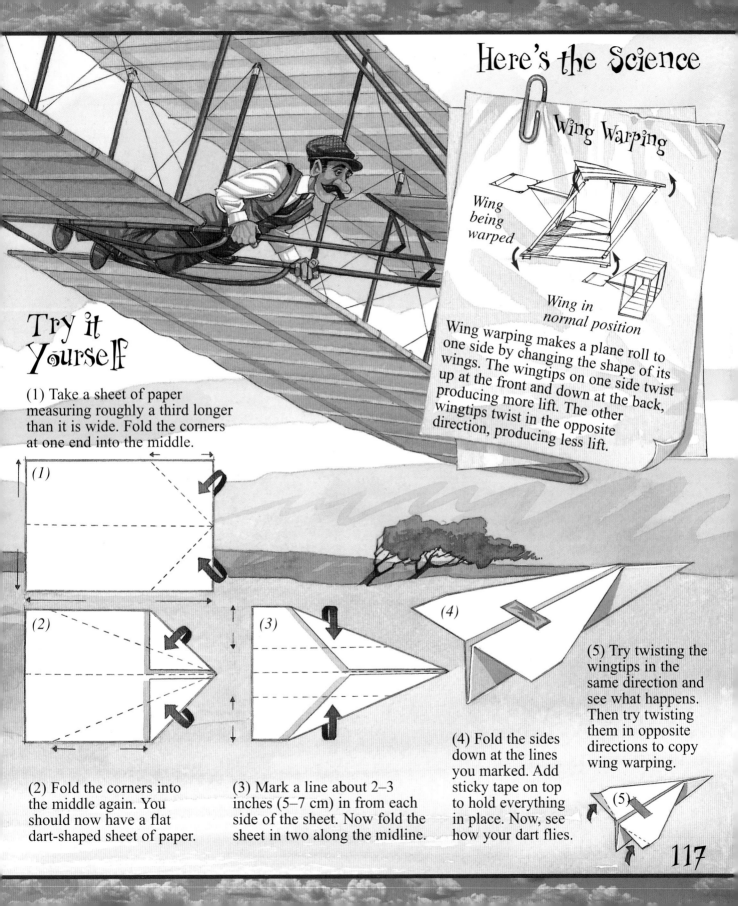

Here's the Science

Wing Warping

Wing warping makes a plane roll to one side by changing the shape of its wings. The wingtips on one side twist up at the front and down at the back, producing more lift. The other wingtips twist in the opposite direction, producing less lift.

Wing being warped

Wing in normal position

Try it Yourself

(1) Take a sheet of paper measuring roughly a third longer than it is wide. Fold the corners at one end into the middle.

(1)

(2)

(2) Fold the corners into the middle again. You should now have a flat dart-shaped sheet of paper.

(3)

(3) Mark a line about 2–3 inches (5–7 cm) in from each side of the sheet. Now fold the sheet in two along the midline.

(4)

(4) Fold the sides down at the lines you marked. Add sticky tape on top to hold everything in place. Now, see how your dart flies.

(5) Try twisting the wingtips in the same direction and see what happens. Then try twisting them in opposite directions to copy wing warping.

(5)

117

Back to the Drawing Board

You and your brother realise that you can't rely on facts and figures from other people, so you decide to do your own research. In 1901 you go home to Dayton with notes on the flights you have made that year. You build all sorts of devices to test different shapes of wings. As you don't have much money, everything is built using whatever materials, tools and equipment are already on hand. This includes a test machine made from a bicycle and a wind tunnel made from a wooden box, a fan, and your workshop motor. Armed with your own research results, you start work on designing a completely new glider.

BICYCLE TEST RIG. The bicycle has an extra wheel on top with a flat plate on one side and a model wing, standing on end, on the other side. As the bicycle is ridden, wind hits the plate and the wing tries to turn the wheel in opposite directions. By trying different model wings and seeing how much the wheel turns, you can tell which wing is best.

Flat plate

Model wing

Bicycle test rig

Wind tunnel

WIND TUNNEL. The most useful of your test machines is a wind tunnel. A fan blows air through it at approximately 30 mph (48 kph), so that you can test different-shaped wings.

Here's the Science

Stalling

Direction of flight

If a plane's nose tips up too far, air cannot flow smoothly over its wings. Lift suddenly disappears and the plane dives. This is called 'stalling'.

Wright brothers' workshop

Perfection!

No. 3 *glider*

n 1902 you and Wilbur go back to Kitty Hawk with a new glider, your *No. 3*. This has been designed using the results of your latest research and tests. Its wings are longer and thinner than earlier gliders and it has two tall vanes at the back. It flies better than your previous designs, but there are still a few problems to iron out. You find it flies better with the wingtips a little closer together, and the tail needs some changes to make it easier to control in turns. By the time you've finished with it, *No. 3* is the world's first fully controllable aircraft. It is so successful that you decide you are ready to move on to the next step – building a powered aircraft.

THE *No. 3* WRIGHT GLIDER of 1902 looks slender and graceful because of its longer, thinner wings (above). After all the research that went into its design, it flies beautifully too.

However, *No. 3* can be tricky in turns. In one, it slides sideways and slams into the ground. Luckily, as the pilot, you are dazed but uninjured.

Daze   (OH!)   Spin   (OH!)

I think we need to look at the tail.

Pitch, Roll and Yaw

An aircraft can move in three different ways – pitch, roll and yaw.

YAW. An aircraft yaws when its nose turns to the left or right.

PITCH. An aircraft's pitch changes when its nose rises or falls.

ROLL. An aircraft rolls, or banks, when one wing rises and the other falls.

TURNING PROBLEM. You discuss how to solve the problem of sliding in turns by changing the glider's tail.

RUDDER. You decide to change the tail so that it has one movable vane, a rudder (right), instead of two fixed vanes, to give the pilot more control in turns.

THE TAIL is finally linked to the wing-warping cradle (below). Now, when the glider rolls, the tail swivels automatically and keeps the aircraft under control. Perfection!

Wing-warping cradle

Elevator control

Bonk!

Rudder swivels when wings warp

121

Power

It is calculated that you need an 8-horsepower engine weighing up to 181 pounds (82 kg) to power your new aircraft. You think you will be able to buy one from one of the many engine-making companies you know. But when the time comes, you can't get what you want. So, you decide to build the engine yourselves! Your bicycle mechanic, Charles Taylor, helps with the design and then builds it for you. It has four cylinders and burns ordinary petrol. It is ready for testing in only six weeks. Your engine is good enough for the short test-flights you are planning – if your aircraft takes off!

WANTED: ONE ENGINE. You write to suppliers with details of the engine you need. But none is able to supply the right engine at the right price.

BUILD IT YOURSELF. Your mechanic, Charles Taylor, builds your engine without any detailed plans (above). You sketch the parts you need and Taylor makes them. Amazingly, it actually works!

Here's the Science

Petrol Engine

Cylinder

Piston

Shaft

When a petrol engine starts, petrol is sprayed into each of its cylinders. A spark makes the fine mist of petrol burn. The gases produced heat up and expand. They push a piston down the cylinder. The up–down movements of the pistons turn the shaft.

SUCCESS! The finished engine is lighter and more powerful than you expected. Because of this, you are able to make the plane heavier and stronger and it will still take off – you hope!

Engine made by Charles Taylor and the Wright brothers

123

Spinning Props

An engine cannot fly an aeroplane by itself. A propeller is needed to push an aircraft through the air. You and Wilbur think you can simply redesign ship propellers to produce a propeller that works in air. But you are amazed to find that ship propellers are made by trial and error! You first have to work out how ship propellers function before designing your own propellers. You decide to use two, driven by chains from the engine. Mounting the propellers behind the wings means that they won't spoil the smooth airflow over the wings.

So why are they this shape, Orville?

You have a terrible temper!

What do you mean, I have a terrible temper?

ARGUMENTS. You and your brother are great arguers. You often thrash out tricky problems by shouting at each other at the tops of your voices!

SHIP PROPELLERS. You both want to base your airplane propellers on ship propellers. The trouble is, no-one has worked out how to design them. Even the people who make ship propellers don't know why they are the shape they are!

THE WRIGHT PROPELLERS ARE TESTED (below) to make sure your theories and calculations are correct. Each wooden propeller is 9 feet (2.6 m) from tip to tip.

They don't seem to know, Wilbur!

Here's the Science

How a Propeller Works

A propeller is like a set of whirling wings. As its blades cut through air, the air pressure drops in front and rises behind, forcing the plane through the sky.

Propeller

Whirr

Building the Flyer

Y ou and your brother's first powered aircraft, the *Flyer*, has a wooden frame and a wingspan of 40 feet (12.3 m). There are two elevators at the front and two rudders at the back. The wings, elevators and rudders are covered with fabric. The engine is mounted on the lower wing. But there is still no seat! The pilot lies in a cradle that slides from side to side to warp the wings. There are no wheels either. The *Flyer* rests on a trolley on a long rail. When the plane takes off, the trolley falls away. When it lands again, it simply skids to a halt on the ground.

Flyer

Well, it's taken four years...

Let's hope it works!

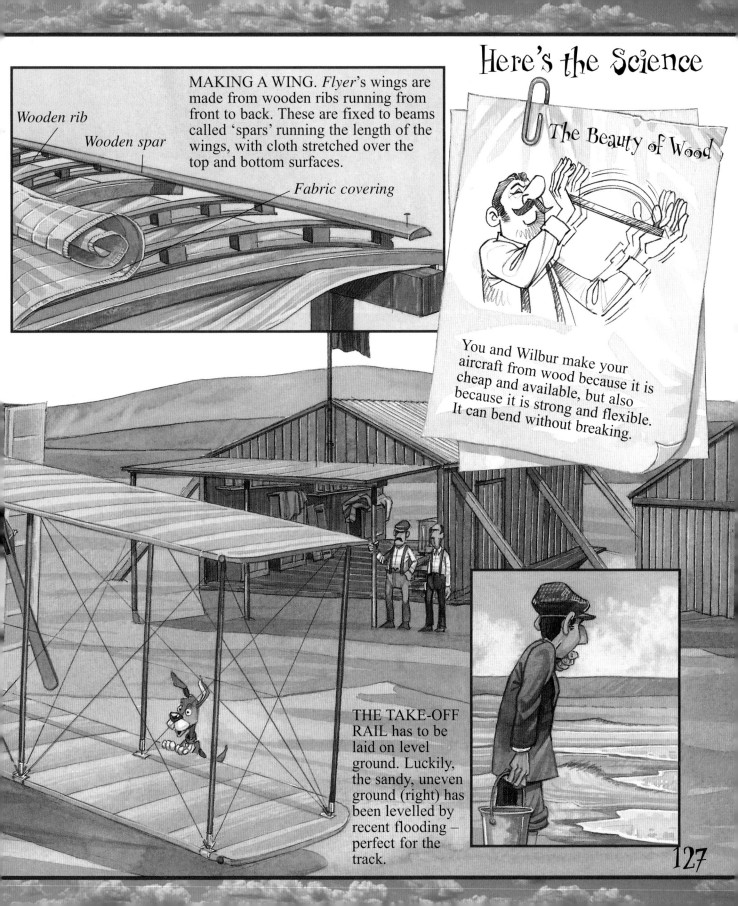

MAKING A WING. *Flyer*'s wings are made from wooden ribs running from front to back. These are fixed to beams called 'spars' running the length of the wings, with cloth stretched over the top and bottom surfaces.

Wooden rib

Wooden spar

Fabric covering

The Beauty of Wood

You and Wilbur make your aircraft from wood because it is cheap and available, but also because it is strong and flexible. It can bend without breaking.

THE TAKE-OFF RAIL has to be laid on level ground. Luckily, the sandy, uneven ground (right) has been levelled by recent flooding – perfect for the track.

127

The First Flight...Ever!

Preparations for the first flight are made on the morning of 14 December 1903. You toss a coin to decide who will pilot the *Flyer*. Wilbur wins. He lies down in the warp cradle and the engine is started. The plane moves away down the launch rail, gathers speed, and lifts off. Then disaster! It ploughs into the sand! It is 17 December before you can try again. It is your turn to be pilot. Five other people witness this attempt. This time, the plane sails away into the wind and lands 12 seconds later, aproximately 120 feet (36 m) away. You make three more flights that day. You have made history!

THE FIRST ATTEMPT to make a flight fails and the plane is damaged. Wilbur, who is piloting the plane, is unhurt.

I've never used a camera before!

START THE ENGINE. The plane is held while the engine starts. When it reaches full speed, the plane is released.

GET READY. You lend your camera to one of the witnesses, John Daniels, who aims it at the position where the *Flyer* is expected to leave the ground.

Image of the first flight, 17 December 1903

Daniels presses the button at the right moment to take a historic photograph (similar to the image above) of the first-ever aeroplane flight!

Here's the Science

Aeroplane Forces

Lift

Drag

Thrust

Weight

The same four forces act on all aeroplanes, including the Wright *Flyer*: weight, lift, thrust and drag.

Lift from the wings pulls the plane upward; thrust from the propellers pushes the plane forward; drag, or air resistance, tries to slow the plane down; weight due to gravity pulls the plane down.

They done it! They done it!

And Now, Next Year's Model

Flyer II *at Huffman Aerodrome, USA*

Making history would be enough for most people, but not Wilbur and Orville Wright! Now you build a series of new planes, each improving on the one before. The first is *Flyer II*, built in 1904. Engine power means that you don't need strong winds to take off, so you leave Kitty Hawk and start flying at Huffman Prairie, closer to your home in Dayton. In 1905 you build *Flyer III*. This is the first really practical aeroplane, and you finally have an aircraft that can make longer flights. You can bank, turn, fly in circles, make figures of eight, whatever you want. *Flyer III*'s longest flight lasts for 38 minutes.

FLYER II. You use *Flyer II* to learn how to control a plane in the air. Then you think you can improve on it. So you build yet another plane and call it *Flyer III*!

THE END OF THE ORIGINAL FLYER. Later in the same day as its first historic flights, the original *Flyer* is hit by a gust of wind. John Daniels tries to hold it down, but it turns over, injuring him. *Flyer* is damaged so badly that it never flies again.

Spot the Difference

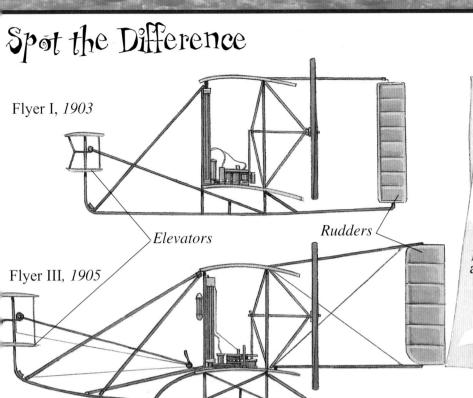

Flyer I, *1903*

Flyer III, *1905*

Elevators

Rudders

Compared to the original *Flyer*, *Flyer III* has its elevators further forward and its rudders further back. Making the plane longer makes it easier for the pilot to control it.

Here's the Science

Pulleys

Pulleys are useful for changing the direction of a force. You and Wilbur use them to change the down, or vertical, force of a weight into a side, or horizontal, force to pull an aircraft along its launch rail.

Vertical force

Horizontal force

RAISING THE LAUNCH-SYSTEM WEIGHT. Before each flight, the 1,760-pound (800 kg) weight has to be raised to the top of the tower (right). It is usually done by a group of volunteers pulling on a rope. Then the rope is hooked up to the plane.

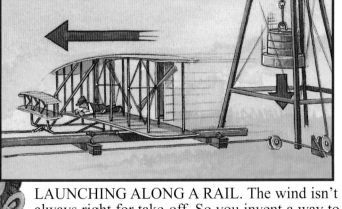

LAUNCHING ALONG A RAIL. The wind isn't always right for take-off. So you invent a way to take off that doesn't rely on the wind. A falling weight (above) tugs a rope that pulls the aeroplane along its launch-rail.

Launch system with weight, pulleys and rail

Look! He's flying!

131

Take a Seat

In 1907 you and your brother finally build an aeroplane with a seat! The *Type A*, as it becomes known, is an improved version of *Flyer III*. Not only does it have a seat for the pilot, but also a passenger seat. The first aeroplane passengers experience the magic of flight in 1908. They sit on the wing with the pilot, so it is a very windy experience. That can cause problems, because of the fashion of the day. Any woman who flies as a passenger has to have her long skirt tied around with string to preserve her modesty! Now that the pilot is sitting up and not lying in a warp cradle, he can't slide to each side to warp the wings and bank (roll) the plane. Instead, he uses control sticks to move the rudders, wings and elevators.

Flight Controls

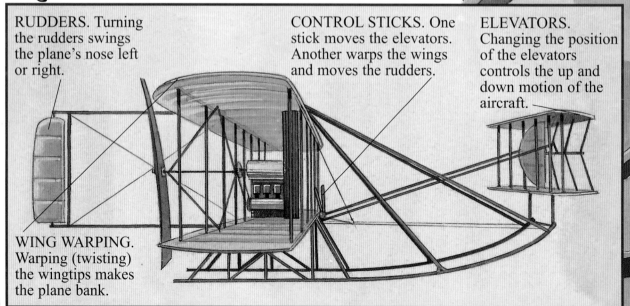

RUDDERS. Turning the rudders swings the plane's nose left or right.

CONTROL STICKS. One stick moves the elevators. Another warps the wings and moves the rudders.

ELEVATORS. Changing the position of the elevators controls the up and down motion of the aircraft.

WING WARPING. Warping (twisting) the wingtips makes the plane bank.

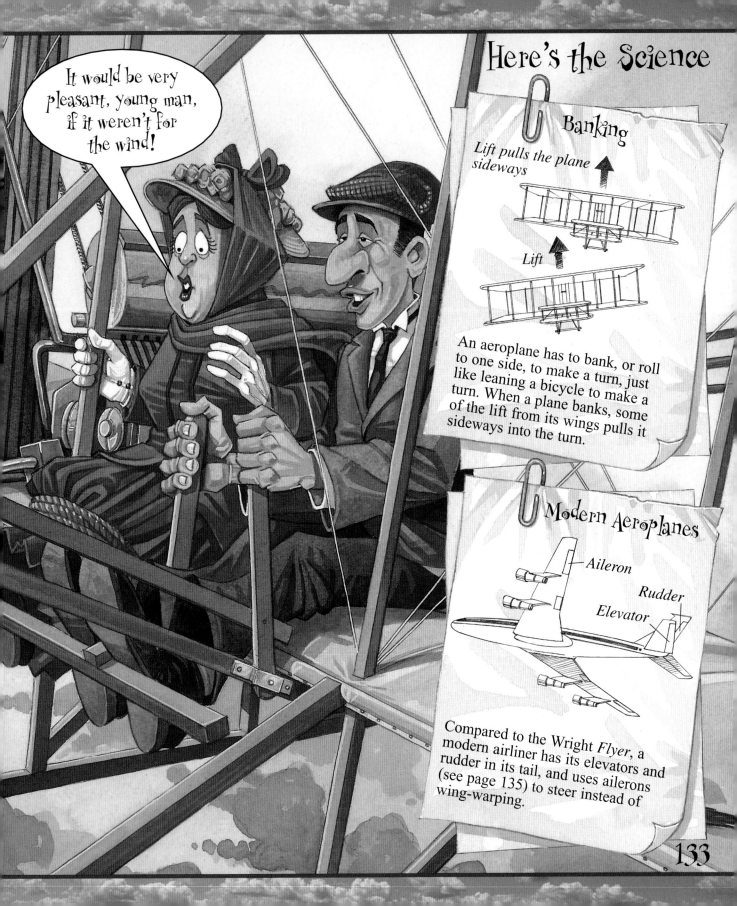

Here's the Science

Banking

Lift pulls the plane sideways

Lift

An aeroplane has to bank, or roll to one side, to make a turn, just like leaning a bicycle to make a turn. When a plane banks, some of the lift from its wings pulls it sideways into the turn.

Modern Aeroplanes

Aileron

Rudder

Elevator

Compared to the Wright *Flyer*, a modern airliner has its elevators and rudder in its tail, and uses ailerons (see page 135) to steer instead of wing-warping.

133

Showing the World

Y ou and your brother show the world your invention in 1908. Wilbur makes flights in France, while you show the plane to the US Army. (The army was offered a Wright plane in 1905, but they thought the idea of military aircraft was ridiculous!) All goes well until you take Lieutenant T. E. Selfridge up for a flight. Disaster strikes – you crash and Selfridge is killed. The army buys the plane anyway.

Meanwhile, in France, people don't believe reports of the Wright brothers' success. When they see Wilbur flying so gracefully, they are amazed. Count de La Vaulx says the Wright plane has 'revolutionised the aviator's world'.

WILBUR'S FLIGHTS IN FRANCE are front-page news everywhere. This magazine cover (above) shows him flying at Hunaudières Racecourse, near Le Mans, in 1908.

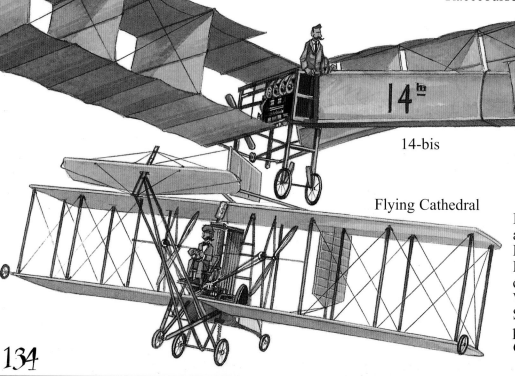

14-bis

Flying Cathedral

EUROPEAN AVIATORS are years behind you. In France, Alberto Santos-Dumont builds an odd plane called *14-bis*. In Britain, the Wild West showman Colonel S. F. Cody is flying a huge plane nicknamed the *Flying Cathedral*!

The World's First Crash Investigation   Here's the Science

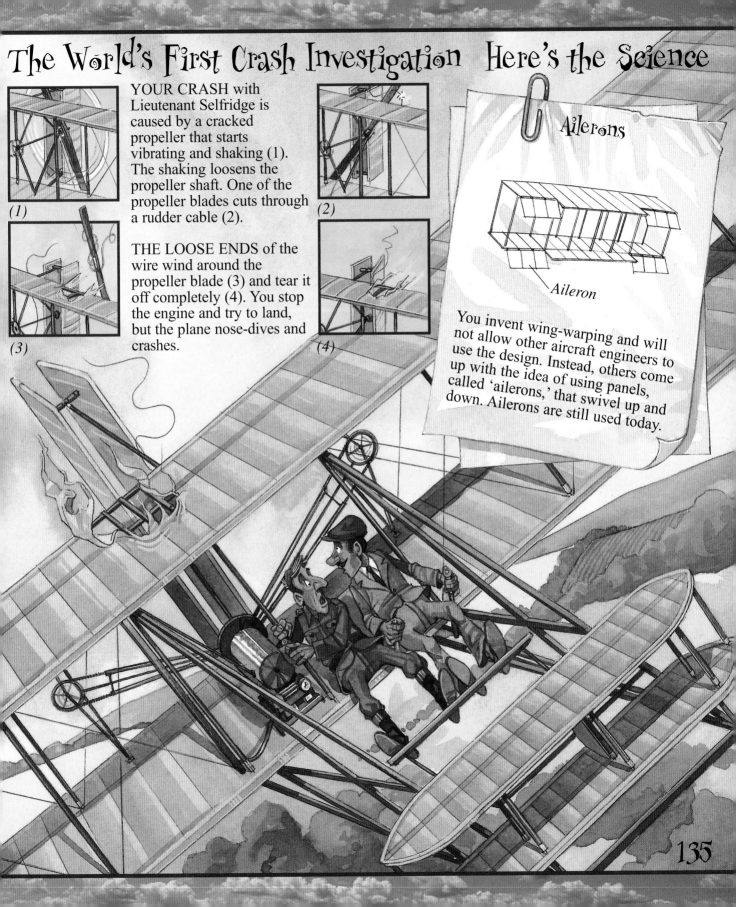

YOUR CRASH with Lieutenant Selfridge is caused by a cracked propeller that starts vibrating and shaking (1). The shaking loosens the propeller shaft. One of the propeller blades cuts through a rudder cable (2).

(1)

(2)

THE LOOSE ENDS of the wire wind around the propeller blade (3) and tear it off completely (4). You stop the engine and try to land, but the plane nose-dives and crashes.

(3)

(4)

Ailerons

Aileron

You invent wing-warping and will not allow other aircraft engineers to use the design. Instead, others come up with the idea of using panels, called 'ailerons,' that swivel up and down. Ailerons are still used today.

135

Glossary

Ailerons Parts of an aircraft's wings that swivel up or down to make the plane roll or bank.

Airfoil The special shape of a wing, designed to produce lift.

Alpha particle A type of particle given out by some radioactive elements. It is made from four smaller particles: two protons and two neutrons.

Amber The hard yellowish-brown fossilised resin of pine trees, known to the ancient Greeks as *elektron*.

Amputation Cutting off a diseased or injured limb.

Anatomy The branch of science that deals with the structure of the body, including the bones in the skeleton, how the muscles are attached to them, and what the major organs are like.

Anemometer An instrument for measuring wind speed.

Antiseptic A substance that kills germs.

Apprentice Someone who is learning a craft, trade or profession.

Arc lamp The electric light invented by Humphry Davy in 1812, which gives off a bright spark between carbon-tipped wires.

Astrology Predicting the future by looking at the positions of the stars.

Atom The smallest particle of an element that can take part in a chemical reaction.

Aviator An old-fashioned word for a flier or pilot.

Banking Rolling an aircraft over to one side to make a turn.

Barber surgeon A general doctor who treated the sick by doing minor operations and recommending herbal potions. The name comes from before Tudor times, when this role was taken by a man who also cut hair, trimmed beards and extracted teeth.

Battery A device containing two substances that react chemically to produce electricity.

Beta particle A type of particle given out by some radioactive elements. A beta particle is an electron produced when a neutron decays, leaving a proton behind.

Bile A green, bitter liquid produced by a small gland just below the liver.

Cancer An illness caused by cells multiplying out of control. Cancer can be caused by the damaging effects of radiation on living cells.

Capacitor A device for storing electric charge.

Carbon A common natural material – coal, charcoal and diamonds are forms of carbon.

Cataract A milky skin that forms on the eyes, particularly in older people. It can cause blindness.

Cells Small units that make up the living tissue of animals and plants; also, a chemical device for making electricity.

Charge An amount of electricity.

Chemical reaction A process in which two or more substances combine to make different substances.

Circuit The complete path taken by an electrical current along a suitable conductor.

Clinometer An instrument for measuring how steep a slope is.

Code A system for changing one kind of information (such as sounds) into another (such as electrical signals).

Conductor A substance that allows electricity to flow through it easily.

Current The flow of electrons along a conductor.

Cylinder The tube-shaped part inside a petrol engine where the fuel is burned.

Decay The change of a radioactive nucleus into a different nucleus by giving out particles or energy waves, resulting in a new isotope.

Diagnosis Identification of a patient's illness by looking at the symptoms.

Diameter The measurement across the widest part of a circle.

Diaphragm A flexible layer, like a skin, which vibrates in air and in a microphone that can send and receive sound waves.

Digital switching A way of changing continuous electrical current into a sequence of '0' and '1' ('on–off') electrical signals.

Dissection Cutting up a dead body to study what is inside.

Drag A force that tries to slow down an aircraft, caused by air pressing against the aircraft as it flies along.

Ducking stool A low stool attached to a frame. In Tudor times, a form of punishment was to be put on the stool and ducked underneath the water of a lake or pond.

Electrode A metal or some other conductor that allows electrical current to pass in or out of an electrical device.

Electromagnet A magnet that works only when a current passes through a coil of wire wrapped around an iron core.

Electron The part of an atom that carries a negative (–) electrical charge.

Element The simplest form of a substance that can take part in chemical reactions.

Elevator The part of an aircraft that tilts to make the plane climb or dive.

Elocution The study of speech and teaching people to speak properly.

Essence A substance made from plants and flowers by boiling them up and concentrating the resulting liquid.

Fever A raised body temperature. Severe fevers can be very dangerous and even deadly.

Fibre optics The method of sending light-signals at very high speed through thin glass or plastic tubes bundled together.

Frequency The number of (sound) waves produced within a given period of time. The frequency of a sound wave determines its pitch. The greater the frequency of a sound wave, the higher the pitch.

Friction The force that acts on one surface rubbing against another.

Gamma ray One type of radiation given out by a radioactive nucleus in the form of a wave, like radio or light, but with much shorter waves.

Gauze A netlike mesh of wire.

Generator A machine for making electricity from mechanical energy.

Glider An aircraft designed to fly without an engine.

Half-life The time taken for half of the atoms of a radioactive element to decay once.

Harmonic telegraph A device in which an electric current carries notes or sounds.

Herbalism The treating of illness using mixtures and preparations of herbs.

Infusion A liquid prepared by boiling a plant or herb, and given to a patient as a health-giving drink.

Insulator Any material that blocks the flow of electrical current.

Iron filings Tiny pieces of iron, easily affected by a magnet.

Isotopes Different forms of the same element made from atoms with different numbers of neutrons in their nucleus. Some isotopes are radioactive.

Laboratory A place where scientists work and carry out experiments.

Leeches Small, sluglike animals that suck blood.

Leukemia A type of cancer that affects the blood. More and more white blood cells are produced while the number of red blood cells decreases.

Lift The upward force produced by a wing that makes an aeroplane rise into the air.

Magnetic field The lines of force around the poles of a magnet.

Magnetism The invisible force that attracts some metals and is given out by an electric current as well as by some substances.

Mallet A blunt wooden hammer. Surgeons once used one to knock out patients who needed serious surgery, such as a leg amputation.

Midwife A nurse who looks after a woman while she gives birth to a baby.

Modem A device that links a computer to the phone network in the Internet.

Musket A long-barrelled gun.

Neutron One of the three particles that atoms are made from. Neutrons are found inside an atom's nucleus. Not all atoms have neutrons. A neutron has no electric charge. A neutron can change into a proton by giving out a beta particle.

Nucleus The particle, or particles, at the centre of an atom.

Opium A drug made from poppies.

Particles The tiny parts inside an atom.

Patent An inventor's description of a new invention, filed at a patent office so that no other inventor can copy the same invention.

Phlegm The gooey substance produced by the lungs and linings of the nose and throat.

Photoelectric cell A device for turning light into electrical energy.

Pike A long, spearlike weapon used by 16th-century soldiers.

Pioneer Someone who is among the first to do something.

Piston Part of a petrol engine that moves up and down inside a cylinder and turns the engine's main shaft.

Pitch A movement of an aircraft that makes its nose rise or fall.

Pitchblende A type of rock that contains uranium. Marie Curie discovered radium and polonium in this material.

Plague A disease spread by fleas on rats that caused many deaths during the 14th, 15th and 16th centuries.

Platinum A rare and expensive metal that is very resistant to corrosion.

Polonium One of the two new elements discovered by Marie Curie in pitchblende.

Proton The part of an atom that carries a positive (+) electrical charge.

Radiation The particles and wave energy given out by a radioactive substance. Other waves, including radio, light, and X-rays, are also called radiation.

Radio A form of radiation, used to send sounds through the air without wires.

Radioactivity The breakdown of a radioactive element by giving out alpha or beta particles or gamma rays.

Radium One of the two new elements discovered by Marie Curie in pitchblende.

Remedy A treatment.

Resistance The amount of opposition a material has to the flow of electric current through it.

Rib Part of the frame inside a wing that runs from the front of the wing to the back.

Roll A movement of an aircraft that makes one wing rise and the other fall.

Rudder The part of an aeroplane's tail that swivels from side to side to make the plane's nose turn to the left or right.

Satellite A spacecraft held in orbit around a planet by gravity.

Shaft A spinning rod in an engine.

Solar power Using the sun's rays to produce energy.

Spar Part of the frame of an aeroplane's wing that runs the length of the wing.

Stall A sudden loss of lift caused by flying too slowly or raising an aircraft's nose too high.

Static electricity An electric charge that is not moving.

Steam engine A machine using steam from a heated-water boiler to drive pistons and turn wheels.

Technology Science put to practical use, using systems and equipment made by inventors.

Telegraph A communications system for sending messages, invented in an electrical form in the 1830s (earlier systems used moving flags, levers or lights).

Thrust The force that pushes an aeroplane through the air.

Transmutation The change of one type of atom to another by radioactive decay.

Trepanning The practice of cutting a hole in a human skull to relieve pressure or let out evil spirits.

Tumour A growth caused by cells dividing and multiplying out of control.

Tuning fork A two-pronged metal fork used by musicians to sound a note.

Vane An aircraft part in the shape of a fin or flat panel.

Variable current An electric current that changes strength, and so can produce different effects in a linked apparatus.

Vibrations Fast movements, up and down or from side to side.

Warp cradle The wooden frame that the pilot of a Wright glider lay in and slid to one side or the other to make the aircraft bank.

Wind tunnel A tube or chamber through which air is blown by a fan, to test wings and other aircraft parts.

Wing Part of an aircraft designed to produce lift when it cuts through air.

Wing warping Twisting a plane's wingtips to make it roll or bank.

X-rays Energy waves similar to radio waves and light waves but much shorter; produced when fast-moving electrons hit a hard material.

Yaw A movement of an aircraft that makes its nose turn to the right or left.

Index

Radium Institute 102, 104, 106, 109
radon 101
ribs 126, 136
Roentgen, Wilhelm 88
roll 121, 136
Royal Court 13
Royal Institution 36, 40, 44, 100
Royal Society 101
rudder 121, 131, 132, 135, 137
Rutherford, Ernest 56, 89

S

safety 37, 55
sailors 28
Santos-Dumont, Alberto 134
scrofula 18
scurvy 28
seasickness 29
Selfridge, Lt T. E. 134
sievert (unit of measurement) 109
smoking 31
solar power 54, 59
soldiers 14, 16, 17, 20
Sorbonne, The 102
sound waves 60
Spanish Armada 28, 30
spars 126, 137
speaking tube 67
St Vitus's Dance 18
stalling 119, 137
static electricity 35, 59
steam engines 52, 59
string phone 65
Strowger, Almon 76
Sturgeon, William 44

Sullivan, Anne 79
sulphuric acid 70
Swan, Joseph 52
switchboard, automatic 76
switchboard operators 74

T

take-off rail 126, 127, 128, 131
Taylor, Charles 122
telegraph 60, 62, 63
telephone 70, 72, 74
  exchange 74, 75
testgear 118–119
thorium 91, 101
thrust 129, 137
toads 14
tooth extractions 20, 32
Transatlantic cable 82
transformers 57, 59
transmutation 101
trepanning 20, 33
tuberculosis 108
tuning fork 64, 67
Twain, Mark 77
Type A aircraft 132

U

University of Paris 102
uranium 88, 90, 91, 94, 101
urine 8–9, 32, 33
US Army 134
US Weather Bureau 115

V

variable current 71
Vaulx, Count de La 134
velocipede 50

Vesalius, Andreas 10
vibrations 60, 63
Victoria, Queen 56, 72, 73
Visual Speech 62, 64
vocal cords 63
Volta, Alessandro 38

W

war 16, 20, 28–29
warp cradle 126, 128, 132, 137
warts 14
Watson, Thomas 68, 70
weapons 14, 16, 28, 33
weight 129, 131
Wheatstone, Sir Charles 62
wheels 126
Whitgift, Archbishop 30
Williams, Charles 68
willow bark 24, 25
wind tunnel 118, 119, 137
wing warping 116, 117, 121, 132, 135, 137
wings 114, 118, 119, 120, 121, 124, 126, 132, 137
witchcraft 22
Wollaston, William 43
Wright, Orville 112–113, 116, 120, 128, 130, 134, 135
Wright, Wilbur 112–113, 128, 130, 134

X

X-rays 88, 89, 104, 105, 108

Y

yaw 121, 137